Revitalizing Teaching Through Faculty Development

Paul A. Lacey, *Editor*

NEW DIRECTIONS FOR TEACHING AND LEARNING
KENNETH E. EBLE and JOHN F. NOONAN, *Editors-in-Chief*

Number 15, September 1983

Paperback sourcebooks in
The Jossey-Bass Higher Education Series

Jossey-Bass Inc., Publishers
San Francisco • Washington • London

Paul A. Lacey (Ed.).
Revitalizing Teaching Through Faculty Development.
New Directions for Teaching and Learning, no. 15.
San Francisco: Jossey-Bass, 1983.

New Directions for Teaching and Learning Series
Kenneth E. Eble and John F. Noonan, *Editors-in-Chief*

New Directions for Teaching and Learning is published quarterly
by Jossey-Bass Inc., Publishers. Subscriptions, single-issue
orders, change of address notices, undelivered copies, and other
correspondence should be sent to *New Directions* Subscriptions,
Jossey-Bass Inc., Publishers, 433 California Street, San Francisco,
California 94104.

Editorial correspondence should be sent to the Editors-in-Chief,
Kenneth E. Eble or John F. Noonan, Center for Improving
Teaching Effectiveness, Virginia Commonwealth University,
Richmond, Virginia 23284.

Library of Congress Catalogue Card Number LC 82-84209
International Standard Serial Number ISSN 0271-0633
International Standard Book Number ISBN 87589-950-1

Cover art by Willi Baum
Manufactured in the United States of America

Ordering Information

The paperback sourcebooks listed below are published quarterly and can be ordered either by subscription or single-copy.

Subscriptions cost $35.00 per year for institutions, agencies, and libraries. Individuals can subscribe at the special rate of $21.00 per year *if payment is by personal check.* (Note that the full rate of $35.00 applies if payment is by institutional check, even if the subscription is designated for an individual.) Standing orders are accepted. Subscriptions normally begin with the first of the four sourcebooks in the current publication year of the series. When ordering, please indicate if you prefer your subscription to begin with the first issue of the *coming* year.

Single copies are available at $7.95 when payment accompanies order, and *all single-copy orders under $25.00 must include payment.* (California, New Jersey, New York, and Washington, D.C., residents please include appropriate sales tax.) For billed orders, cost per copy is $7.95 plus postage and handling. (Prices subject to change without notice.)

Bulk orders (ten or more copies) of any individual sourcebook are available at the following discounted prices: 10–49 copies, $7.15 each; 50–100 copies, $6.35 each; over 100 copies, *inquire.* Sales tax and postage and handling charges apply as for single copy orders.

To ensure correct and prompt delivery, all orders must give either the *name of an individual* or an *official purchase order number.* Please submit your order as follows:

Subscriptions: specify series and year subscription is to begin.
Single Copies: specify sourcebook code (such as, TL8) and first two words of title.

Mail orders for United States and Possessions, Latin America, Canada, Japan, Australia, and New Zealand to:
Jossey-Bass Inc., Publishers
433 California Street
San Francisco, California 94104

Mail orders for all other parts of the world to:
Jossey-Bass Limited
28 Banner Street
London EC1Y 8QE

New Directions for Teaching and Learning Series
Kenneth E. Eble and John F. Noonan, *Editors-in-Chief*

Contents

Editor's Notes

This sourcebook seeks to encourage faculty and administrators who are concerned about revitalizing college teaching. In the following chapters, a handful of teachers describe what they have done to strengthen their own teaching and the commitment of their institutions to teaching. Each author has participated in a foundation-funded program for postdoctoral teaching fellows at his or her university. Each university's program has certain common features: Fellows are junior faculty in the third or fourth year of teaching, except in a few cases where the university chooses to support the participation of senior faculty members through its own funds; each fellow must receive released time or compensated time to work on a teaching and learning project, which is often connected with designing a course or a new teaching method; and each university must contribute to the program by providing administrative support, consultants or mentors, and access to other institutional resources. The university programs must also have some pattern, appropriate to their own needs and ethos, for bringing fellows together regularly and working closely with them. The grant is not simply a convenient way to let each person go his own way in isolation. In fact, Lilly Endowment, Inc., which offers the grants, believes it is valuable for academics to meet and talk with one another about their common concerns and interests. It sponsors two conferences each year for all participants from each university program, in which consultants and speakers make presentations, lead discussions, and engage informally with the fellows and directors.

Taken together, the chapters throw light on a range of questions about how better teaching can be encouraged. The authors describe how they developed new courses, worked through the intellectual problems of identifying course goals and objectives, specified and organized content, orchestrated assignments and experiences so that students built up both their skills and their understanding of content, and shaped the teaching and learning milieu in order to accomplish a larger and more carefully specified number of purposes.

The chapters that describe developing a new course or a new emphasis in a course take us through the problem-solving process and show us what comes out of it for the benefit of the student and the instructor. In Chapter One, Beverly A. P. Taylor describes how she developed a pre-physics course to meet the educational needs of a spe-

1

cific kind of underprepared student: the kind who wants a career in science and has gotten by to a certain point on memorizing right answers, but cannot go any farther without learning how to think through a problem to discover the answer. To meet the needs of those students, Taylor studied the way people learn scientific reasoning — for example, how they go from direct experience to generalization and abstraction — and then how they can best be taught — for example, how questioning can lead them step by step from an observation to a conclusion about it. She describes several important interconnected processes that are involved in her creation of the pre-physics course: recognizing that everyone progresses from concrete to formal reasoning abilities in the same way and therefore discovering more about how to teach the advanced as well as the underprepared student; reflecting on what an able person learns when engaged in teaching someone else; and finding that attitudes toward teaching change when it is done effectively. Finally, Taylor reports that the problems of teaching physics are not unique; there are many colleagues in other disciplines with whom one might share problems and insights. Even more importantly, this author notes that caring about teaching, especially in an area like physics, is not the same as a confession that one is incapable of doing "real" research.

Reconceptualization is perhaps the key to all the experiments in course design reported in these chapters. In Chapter Two, Phil Brown sets out to create a multidisciplinary approach to a familiar subject in sociology. He describes ways to use the arts to illuminate séveral different world views of mental illness — not simply by illustrating forms of mental illness but by using the pre-existing concepts people have about it. He describes a course that moves from knowledge about the subject to a sympathetic entrance into several world views of mental illness. He hopes to rephrase fundamental questions in order to learn how daily activities reverberate in people's lives, and this means encouraging students to tap the emotional side of their own lives for new insights. Most fundamentally, he wants to teach his field, sociology — its principles and methods — and his topic of mental illness with scholarly integrity. In the process of reconceptualizing the subject of his course, Phil Brown also discovered that he uses material from his research at the same time that he enriches that research. He discovered new sources of materials for both teaching and research, new teaching methods appropriate to his work, new connections with faculty colleagues, and new uses of the library.

In Chapter Three, Jean Ferguson Carr reconceptualizes an introductory course in English literature to meet the needs of students enrolled in preprofessional and skill-oriented courses of study. Carr conceives of the introductory literature course as one that stresses epistemological relationships among disciplines, rather than one that serves as an entry into a sequence that will lead through intermediate to advanced work in the discipline. The course, *Fiction and Fact,* teaches literary interpretation as a process of inquiry among other processes of inquiry: It considers the relation of a formal discipline to its knowledge, its ways of knowing, and the worlds it describes. Instead of presenting literary texts as finished, ordered products that construct an entire world, this introductory course helps students to see the need for understanding those texts as incomplete world views. There are other ways of ordering and explaining the world — for example, historical, autobiographical, legal, and psychological interpretations — that are also full of gaps. Carr's course therefore seeks to teach students to comprehend how all worlds, including their own, are made up of "interwoven perspectives."

How a teacher can bring a group of beginning students through so complex and potentially threatening a process and then use that process to teach writing, responses to literature, and openness to the multiplicity of worlds represented in a university curriculum is a remarkable story. In the telling, Carr also shows us rich connections between teaching and research.

Curtina Moreland-Young addresses another kind of pedagogical problem, in Chapter Four, that often arises in an introductory course: how to teach students thinking skills that are necessary for the discipline but, at the same time, do justice to the demands of the content of the discipline. Teachers often deal with the frustrations inherent in this problem in unproductive ways. For example, they blame the students — "Why don't they know how to analyze?" They blame the high schools — "Don't they teach them anything?" They blame some other department — "What do you do over there in English, if you don't teach them to write?" Moreland-Young starts at a different point: She asks how one can help a student learn to deal with a body of material analytically. For example, how would one take a student from learning analysis skills to synthesis skills and then on to a sufficient knowledge of a subject so that creative thinking can occur? Moreland-Young's chapter describes both the process by which she conceptualized the issues and appropriate responses to them and some of the specific class exercises she developed to help students learn how to interpret data, how to organize and reorganize to get the fullest significance from the data, and how to frame questions that clarify the raw information with which one is working. Also, since so much of the work of analysis in a discipline like political science typically takes the form of written essays, teaching thinking skills requires the teacher to teach writing as well. As her chapter indicates, the extra work involved in teaching basic composition resulted in improved performance for her students, new writing and pedagogical opportunities for herself, new styles of teaching to experiment with, and new associations with colleagues across the university.

Each of the chapters in this sourcebook is essentially a report of work in progress, but Erich Lear's (Chapter Five) especially deserves that title. His reconceptualizing has taken the form of asking how a delivery system — Computer-Assisted Instruction — might improve a music theory course. His chapter describes how a course becomes changed by the infusion of Computer-Assisted Instruction in music drills. But the larger story involves Lear's pursuit of his own intellectual curiosity in a new area, in which he allows himself to play with new computer languages, new conceptual systems, and new ways of organizing and presenting knowledge. Readers who would like to know how to get acquainted with the educational uses of computers without being overwhelmed by technical material will find Lear's ideas a "user-friendly" introduction. The chapter is also a testimony to the value of collegiality when one is trying out something new. It, along with some of the other chapters, emphasizes the importance of networks of colleagues for sharing information and mutual support.

A number of these chapters discuss what we have come to call *delivery systems* in education: for example, Programmed Self-Instruction, Computer-Assisted Instruction, peer-teaching, audiovisual aids, laboratories, exercises, lectures, and discussion sections. Each can be thought of as parts of a system — the course — that is intended to make available to a group of students materials, methods, skills, demonstrations of techniques and processes for understanding materials, and opportunities to drill and be tested for competence in subject matter. Reconceptualizing a course can take the form of re-examining the subject matter, the delivery system for that subject matter, or the students in the course as the recipients of the subject matter. Behind many discussions of what to teach and how to teach it lie assumptions about what students need and can absorb in a particular course.

The next two chapters focus particularly on how students receive what we teach. In Chapter Six, Carl E. Paternite, a developmental psychologist, describes how his philosophy and teaching methods have changed over the past four years as more and more of his developmental views have found expression in how he teaches. His views — that individuals are "active architects of their worlds" and that the ways in which people make meaning of their worlds change in predictable, sequential patterns over their lives — have had a strong effect on his work as a psychotherapist, in his research, and in the content of his teaching. But Paternite reports that he originally entered college teaching with little attention to the fact that his students are actively engaged in developmental processes that have important implications for the classroom. The chapter recounts how he went from teaching about human development to teaching that content from a developmental perspective. Now Paternite teaches "Adolescent Development" and "Developmental Psychology of the College Student" to people still living through what he is describing, so he presents the courses in ways that validate the personal, intimate meanings the students attach to the material. He takes the developmental heterogeneity of his classes as a positive challenge, and sets out to devise goals, objectives, course designs, and methods that will aid his students in content-mastery in the course and in personal and intellectual development through the medium of the course. Paternite also describes William Perry's developmental scheme, a dominant influence on the thinking of many of the participants in the teaching fellows programs, and the work of a number of researchers who have explored the classroom implications of that work.

Walter L. Barker's experiences, described in Chapter Seven, are paradigmatic of many a senior faculty member's first encounter with college teaching: that is, he was invited to take two sections of a course, with two days' notice, and ushered into the teaching profession with a chairman's kindly "Don't worry. You'll do well." Under those circumstances, the natural teacher, the quick learner, or the person with a lot of good models might indeed do well, but nobody then seemed to have very precise standards for determining what that might mean. In any case, Barker was reckoned an exceptionally fine teacher and was therefore invited into his university's teaching fellows program. The result of that year, as he reports in his chapter, was a radical reconceptualizing of his role in the classroom. He began to distinguish the processes of teaching and learning from the product of knowledge, to recognize the discipline-rooted nature of the pedagogical language he used, and to discover how to make the classroom more of a student-oriented than a content-oriented place. As supervisor of teaching assistants in his department, Barker shares the substance of his experience and the insights of his fellowship year with them. They thus start with a clearer sense of direction and purpose in their teaching, work in a setting where it is valid to take teaching seriously, and have a developing language to describe teaching issues.

The final chapter, by Thomas M. Schwen and Mary Deane Sorcinelli, tells how to organize the larger context of support activities and networks of consultants and administrators so that the individual fellow has the greatest opportunity to be rewarded for good teaching. The program they describe identifies goals for individual participants, for departments, and for the whole institution, therefore emphasizing that the soundest individual goals will have little effect unless they are related to departmental needs and an institutional willingness to support teaching excellence. Departments have to be drawn in to sharing ownership of the teaching fellow's project; the chairperson must support the junior colleague and a mentor must be available to work closely with him or her. Also, the rewards for effective teaching must go to the department as well as to the individual. This means working hard on institution-wide supports for teaching, such as promotion and tenure, teaching awards, and administrative encouragement. The Schwen and Sorcinelli chapter is not an exact blueprint for an ideal program to enhance teaching, since institutions vary too widely for anything to be universally effective. However, it is extremely valuable in identifying all the programmatic considerations to be taken into account and in describing what worked best for them.

Two general characteristics of the chapters in this sourcebook should be emphasized. The authors are extremely practical and also enthusiastic about their subjects. Yet, for many in our profession, being strong on practice is sufficient evidence of being weak on theory. And to be enthusiastic is poor form: We must not seem to care too much for our subject, just as some clergymen avoid talking about God for fear of being taken for pious. But these chapters are intellectually grounded; or, to put it more accurately, their practicality and enthusiasm are rooted in intellectual life. They examine fundamental questions such as how to frame and think through an important intellectual problem and how to vitalize the scholarly and pedagogical aspects of our professional lives in relation to one another. At the same time, the authors challenge our unexamined assumptions and entertain new ideas — with enthusiasm. They invite us to take part in those activities.

Paul A. Lacey
Editor

Paul A. Lacey is Bain-Swiggett Professor of English Literature at Earlham College, Richmond, Indiana. He is author of The Inner War: Forms and Themes in Recent American Poetry *(Fortress, 1972). From 1980 to 1983 he was consultant and director for the Lilly Endowment, Inc.'s postdoctoral teaching fellows program.*

The challenge of teaching college freshmen who lack
formal reasoning skills cannot be met by traditional methods.

Teaching Scientific Reasoning to Underprepared Students

Beverly A. P. Taylor

In the last decade much research has been done by physicists, psychologists, and educators about the ways students learn physics and problem solving, the preconceptions they bring with them to the classroom, and the cognitive developmental level necessary for success in physics (Clement, 1982; Fuller, 1982; Champagne and others, 1980; Fuller and others, 1977; Reif and others, 1976). However, very little of this research has been applied in the classroom. In fact, many physics teachers do not know about these studies, and many others who are familiar with them do not consider the research to be relevant to their own teaching. Prior to my year as a teaching fellow, I belonged to the first group. I knew almost nothing about the research being done into the development of scientific reasoning skills. I had heard of Piaget, but knew nothing about his work. I spent the first part of my fellowship year searching the literature for work that had been done on improving student success in physics. The references cited here represent only a

This material is based on work supported in part by the National Science Foundation under grant no. SER-8160904. Any opinions, findings, and conclusions or recommendations expressed in this publication are those of the author and do not necessarily reflect the views of the National Science Foundation.

P. A. Lacey (Ed.). *Revitalizing Teaching Through Faculty Development.* New Directions for Teaching and Learning, no. 15. San Francisco: Jossey-Bass, September 1983.

small portion of the research that has been done and were selected primarily because they are found in journals to which the average science teacher usually has access. The latter part of my fellowship year was spent in applying some of this research to the development of a course for underprepared college freshmen at Jackson State University in Mississippi.

For many years most scientists believed that reasoning skills were gradually developed during the adolescent period through a mysterious combination of observation and concrete experience, sometimes referred to as *self-regulation* (Wadsworth, 1978; Fuller and others, 1977). In general, scientists felt that these skills could not be taught or even learned in a strict sense, but must be acquired by each individual in a manner applicable only to himself. In Piagetian terms, everyone must progress from concrete to formal reasoning abilities in his own way and there is little that can be done to hasten the process. However, it has now become clear that many students enter college without having developed the reasoning skills necessary for success in university courses, particularly in the sciences (Lawson and Renner, 1975). Educators are now faced with two choices, given that we understand that everyone does not magically acquire these skills some time prior to admission to the university. We can ignore the problem, effectively saying that students who have not developed reasoning skills do not have the potential for college education. Or we can attempt to teach reasoning. Acceptance into a teaching fellowship program marked the beginning of my progress from the first choice to the second.

Development of a "Pre-Physics" Course

Need. Many authors (McKinnon and Renner, 1971; Arons, 1976; Griffiths, 1976) have called attention to a widespread need among college students to develop reasoning skills — such as proportional reasoning, hypothesis building and testing, control of variables, and logical implication — that are required for pursuit of a scientific career. The problem is even more acute at Jackson State University (JSU). Approximately 90 percent of the student body is from Mississippi, which is a primarily rural state and suffers from a shortage of mathematics and science teachers in its schools. Also, many students at JSU are first generation college entrants whose parents often have had neither the training nor motivation to advise them in pursuing a college preparatory track in high school. The physics department offers two introductory physics sequences, one including calculus in its math work and the other only algebra. The failure rate in these courses is very high, and students often do not show significant improvement when they repeat the course. However, success in these courses is essential for progress toward the careers in health science, natural science, or engineering that many of these students have chosen. Several basic deficiencies in student preparation have been identified by the science faculty: a lack of academic experience as a foundation on which the abstractions of science can be built, a weakness in mathematical and verbal skills, students' lack of confidence in their ability to solve problems, and low personal standards for academic achievement. These weaknesses persist in second and third year students as well, which indicates that the standard university courses are not correcting the deficiencies in preparation.

Target Population. As I began the project for my teaching fellowship, my intention was to develop a "pre-physics" course for these students — many of them seniors who could not successfuly complete a standard physics course. (The introductory physics sequences are sophomore courses, but most students postpone them as long as possible.) I hoped to be able to give them sufficient preparation to pass the standard course with a C. The first part of the course would have been spent in mathematics review: powers of ten, exponentials, graphing, solving algebraic equations, and basic trigonometry. Then some basic physics concepts would have been introduced. These topics would not be covered in depth but would be used primarily as a medium for introducing basic problem solving techniques. During the development period, I became convinced that, since the skills necessary for physics were also important in many other areas, students would receive more benefit from such a course as freshmen than as seniors. And, as I became more involved over time, I completely changed the format of the course and the material to be covered.

McDermott and others (1980) have pointed out specific difficulties encountered by many students in learning science: "confusion between two concepts that apply to the same situation; problems with scientific reasoning; inability to reason by analogy and to transfer reasoning to new contexts; and lack of connection between reality and representations" (pp. 136–137). Because of these difficulties, particularly the last two, the standard lecture course that I originally envisioned would have accomplished very little. The students would have continued to memorize rather than reason and would not have been able to transfer what they did learn to the next course. What is needed is instruction in which concrete experience and individual attention foster the development of intellectual skills, study habits, and self-confidence, along with subject matter understanding. The Physics Education Group of the University of Washington has, over the past several years, developed and taught a freshman physics sequence designed to prepare students in the Educational Opportunity Program for mainstream science courses (McDermott and others, 1980). During the last three years I have designed and taught a course based on the modular materials that this group has developed.

Course Logistics. The course meets for four two-hour sessions every week. One additional two-hour session is available for optional tutoring. The course is taught using a modified Personalized Self-Instruction (PSI) system. The students, with individual help available, work sequentially through the materials. This includes reading the text, performing simple experiments, and working exercises. Occasionally group discussions are held to summarize or practice particularly difficult concepts. The students are guided in pacing themselves by fixed examination dates. Exams emphasize the correct use and interpretation of data rather than memorized facts through questions that normally demand an explanation of the reasoning used to obtain an answer. Homework also plays an important part in the instruction of these courses, and as in the examinations, explanations are stressed more than correct answers in problem solving. Each assignment focuses on the reasoning involved in solving a problem in order to convince students that understanding is more important than getting the correct answer. Any homework problems that are done incorrectly must be redone properly and resubmitted. This serves to reinforce the importance placed on correct reasoning and to bolster the students' standards for achievement.

Learning Problems Addressed by the Course

Basic Concepts. One of underprepared students' major problems is their lack of an adequate understanding of basic concepts. They often do not distinguish between the ability to repeat the definition of a concept and actually understanding it. For this reason, the course is taught primarily in the laboratory so that direct experience will always precede generalization and abstraction. Technical terms are introduced only after the concepts that they represent have been explored in the laboratory. For instance, prior to the introduction of the word *density,* the students measure the mass and volume of a number of aluminum objects, calculate the ratio of the mass to the volume, observe that it is the same for all the objects, and learn to interpret the resulting number as the number of grams in each cubic centimeter of the object.

Throughout the course the students are encouraged to reason out their questions for themselves. Initially most students need considerable guidance in order to do this. The instructors try to guide the students through the reasoning process by asking appropriate questions. The experiment that introduces the idea of concentration of a solution is a good example of both the use of the laboratory to precede new concepts and the use of questioning to guide the student's reasoning. In this experiment, the student is shown four beakers containing salt solutions. The beakers contain different amounts of water and of salt. The volume of water can be determined by reading the scale on the beaker and the amount of salt in each beaker is written on a card that is placed in front of each beaker. Students are given samples of each solution and asked to match them with the beakers from which they came by tasting the samples. Most students (about 80 percent) initially match the samples and beaker solutions incorrectly, because they focus only on the total amount of salt in the beaker or on the total amount of water. The following is a typical conversation that might take place as the instructor tries to guide the student to reason through the problem.

Instructor: Please taste the samples and match each with the beaker from which you think it came.

Student: Well, I'm not sure, but I think that's right.

Instructor: OK, explain to me how you made your decisions.

Student: I matched the sample that tasted the saltiest with the beaker that had the most salt in it and the next saltiest with the next largest amount of salt and so on.

Instructor: Does the amount of water in the beaker make any difference?

Student: Yes, I guess it does.

Instructor: Can you think of any way to take the amount of water into account?

Student: I could say that the beaker with the least water is the saltiest, but that can't be right because it also has the least salt.

Instructor: Could you match the samples if all the beakers had the same amount of water?

Student: Yes, then my original solution would work.

Instructor: Can you find the amount of salt in each 100 milliliters or some other constant amount of water?

Student: Oh, I see. I can find the number of grams of salt in each milliliter of water for each beaker, and then the beaker with the most salt per milliliter is the saltiest.

After the student has completed the exercise correctly, the instructor explains that the number they have just calculated is called the *concentration* of the solution. It may seem that the student has not done much independent reasoning here; but, after many experiences of this kind, most students do develop both the reasoning skill and the self-confidence necessary to solve problems on their own. Initially most students resent the questions and complain because no one will tell them the answer. However, by the end of the first semester, I often overhear students using this questioning technique themselves to help another student think through a difficult problem.

The lack of adequate understanding of basic concepts often leads to confusion between related concepts, such as speed and acceleration, heat and temperature, weight and volume, or area and volume. In the laboratory experiments, the students are presented with the opportunity to confuse the concepts, to confront the confusion, and then to separate the ideas on their own. For example, near the beginning of the study of motion, a demonstration is performed for small groups of students in which steel ball bearings are rolled on aluminum tracks. One ball moves at constant speed on a level track and another rolls down an inclined track so that it continually speeds up. The ball on the inclined track is initially behind, then catches up and passes the first ball. The students are asked to identify the point in the motion when the two balls have the same speed. Someone always incorrectly chooses the point at which the balls are side by side. Then the demonstration moves to two sets of level tracks. The students observe two balls moving at the same speed, with one behind the other, and also two balls moving with different constant speeds. In the second case, the faster ball catches up with and passes the slower one, but yet they never have the same speed. After observing the two balls moving with the same speed, most students realize that the distance between the balls remains constant. Then they can return to the original problem and correctly identify the point at which the speeds are the same as being the short time period in which the distance between the two balls appears to remain constant. When presented with a similar situation a few days later, some students will revert to using the criterion of when two moving objects are in the same position. However, after several of these experiments over a period of weeks, most students are able to correctly use the concepts of position, speed, and acceleration.

The materials used for the motion part of the course were developed as a result of a systematic study conducted at the University of Washington, in which student understanding of the concepts of instantaneous velocity and acceleration was tested. Pre- and post-testing of the academically disadvantaged students indicated a marked improvement of their ability to apply these concepts to simple motions of real objects (Trowbridge and McDermott, 1980, 1981).

Analogies. It is important to develop reasoning skills in the context of specific physical examples, because these students are often limited in their ability to reason by analogy and to transfer reasoning skills from one situation to another. In most standard physics classes, analogy is used extensively as a teaching tool: Rotational motion is just like linear motion; heat flow is just like fluid flow; light behaves just like a water wave. The ability to make these analogies must be carefully developed in underprepared students, and should usually be done only after some classroom exposure to specific examples. That is, a student who has mastered proportional reasoning with mass and volume in density problems may not be able to transfer this skill to a motion problem in which distance and time play the same role as mass and volume. However, once he has conquered the motion problem as an entirely new concept, he can usually be led to realize the connection between the two. Only after many experiences of this nature can he begin to learn new ideas by analogies to old ones.

Abstract Representations. Another weakness that is addressed in the course is the inability to make the connection between reality and representations — such as graphs, diagrams, equations, and verbal statements. A student who can state and manipulate the equations for motion with constant acceleration may still be unable to apply them to what happens when the driver of a car hits the brakes. Or a student who can solve a problem using numbers may not be able to solve the same problem using algebraic variables instead of numbers. These difficulties are addressed in several ways. In the salt water experiment discussed previously, students learn to associate the saltiness of the solution with its concentration. In another experiment, the students prepare eight solutions, then plot a graph of the mass of a dissolved chemical in relation to the volume of water. Solutions that have the same concentration (indicated by the color of the solution rather than the taste in this case) are represented by points that lie on the same straight line on the graph. This helps the student associate the concentration with the slope of the line on the graph. As another example, students are encouraged to follow a systematic method of solving problems involving algebraic variables. In this procedure, the student must explain what the algebraic expression on each side of the equation represents physically and why the two expressions are equal.

Problems in the Teaching Method

One obvious difficulty with the teaching methodology described here is the low student-to-faculty ratio that is required. Frequent student–staff interactions are essential for the growth of reasoning skills. At least one instructor for every eight students is necessary for maximum effectiveness. However, very few universities can afford this sort of student-to-faculty ratio, particularly considering the number of entering freshmen in need of such a course. At Jackson State, there are about 200 freshmen every year who indicate interest in science-related careers but are deemed underprepared for the standard introductory courses. Fortunately, students trained as peer instructors can serve just as well as, or in some instances better than, a faculty member to fill the gap. Students are often more willing to ask questions or admit confusion to another student than to a faculty member. In the course described here, several junior and senior physics majors were used successfully as peer instructors. In addition, the reasoning skills of the peer instructors also improved as they were forced to analyze the steps they themselves go through in solving problems in order to help others develop this ability.

Perhaps the most serious difficulty with teaching the course is convincing the students that reasoning is important and that the effort put into improving their skills now will pay off later. In particular, most students were not willing to take the pre-physics course, which required eight hours in class each week, when they could take a remedial chemistry course that required only three in-class hours a week instead — even after both chemistry and physics faculty members discussed the potential benefits of the new course and encouraged students to take it. I believe their resistance was at least in part due to their previous education, in which they had been taught to value learning concrete facts rather than the less definable ability to reason. I see no solution to this problem other than making the course mandatory or changing the elementary and secondary educational systems. In the latter case, the course might be unnecessary in the first place.

Evaluation of the Course

It is difficult to objectively evaluate the success or failure of the course. At this time, only a few of the students have gone on to take the standard introductory chemistry or physics classes. Of these students, some have been quite successful and others have not. The physics department gives a math quiz to all students beginning the introductory physics course in order to determine their level of preparation, and this same exam is given to students in the pre-physics course at the beginning and end of the first semester. Most students showed improvement in their ability to solve simple word problems and algebraic equations. And, on the end-of-semester course evaluations, almost all of the students indicated that they felt both their ability to think through problems and their confidence in their ability to learn difficult material had improved. Subjectively, I saw a significant change in student problem-solving abilities and their willingness to attempt a solution for all of those enrolled in the course. However, no final conclusions can be drawn until more of the students follow up with the standard university science courses.

Evaluation of Professional Development

Teaching Strategies. My year as a teaching fellow brought about changes in both my instructional techniques and my outlook on teaching as a profession. My overall teaching style has improved; I find myself carrying over ideas developed in the pre-physics course to my standard physics courses. I now include some of the lab experiments from the new course in my standard introductory course. I also put more effort into explaining the thought processes behind my solutions to problems. In my early days of teaching and tutoring, I always used the Socratic method to assist students in reasoning out solutions with as little help from me as possible. However, it gradually became easier to just explain the problem and get on with something else. Now, after my experiences in the pre-physics course over the last two years, I have gone back to using the questioning technique with all students who come to my office for help, whether they are freshmen or seniors.

Transition. I began as something of an academic elitist. I was not particularly concerned about students who could not pass beginning courses in physics or physical science; that merely indicated that they were not prepared for college and should not be there. I was aware that part of the problem was inadequately trained elementary and secondary science teachers and that something needed to be done about it, but there is a difference between being aware of a problem and being willing to be part of the solution. Most of all, I wanted to teach physics to students who were prepared and eager to learn.

In addition, I was a "closet" teacher, meaning that I have always been more interested in teaching than in doing research in physics. This put me very much in the minority of physicists (Rigden, 1981), particularly those I had met prior to the Lilly program. The accepted attitude in physics is that one teaches in order to get paid to do research. As a result, I usually was not open about my interest in teaching. But, through the teaching fellows program, I came into contact with other faculty members on campus who were also concerned about teaching. At the semiannual conferences, I discovered that the teaching problems I had were indeed quite similar to those that faculty in other disciplines encountered. I was surprised, because we scientists tend to think that our teaching problems are unique and that someone who teaches English or history cannot possibly understand, much less contribute to a solution. Probably the most significant change was an indirect result of being a teaching fellow. Participating in the program gave me the encouragement I needed to attend my first national meeting of the American Association of Physics Teachers. I met many other physicists there who enjoyed teaching and were involved in doing research on how to teach physics. I discovered that they were not second-rate physicists incapable of doing "real" research, but were people like myself, who were more excited by teaching and teaching problems than by standard physics research problems. I started to take pride in my teaching abilities and to stop feeling guilty about my enjoyment in teaching. Therefore, my changes in outlook were brought about by people: the other fellows, both at JSU and other universities; Dr. L. C. McDermott, who came to our campus as a consultant for my project; and many other physicists across the nation who are also concerned about teaching.

Conflicts. In designing the course described above, I faced a conflict between my desire to help those students who were failing my introductory physics course and a strong feeling that college credit should not be given for work that was not on the level of standard freshman courses. Courses such as "College Algebra" and "College Arithmetic" always seemed inappropriate to me, since these are subjects that should be mastered prior to college. I looked down at both those who took them and those who taught them. Now I found myself thinking about teaching a course that started out more on the level of junior high school physical science than on the level of college physics. I struggled for some time with the decision to offer it for credit with a physics course number. Several of the members of the board of advisers for the teaching fellows program on campus, as well as Dr. McDermott, were influential in the decision-making process. I finally decided that it was not a student's beginning level of preparation that mattered, but whether or not he or she was able to work at standard college level by the end of the course — which certainly would be the case if a student completed the full year sequence. I also realized that, for true learning to occur, one must begin at a place that the student can understand and then work from there. Anything else is a waste of time for both the instructor and the student. I wish that all entering students were fully prepared for college studies. But, given the actual situation at most colleges and universities, I believe we must be willing to help underprepared students catch up. This includes working to help them develop the scientific reasoning skills that were once considered unteachable.

References

Arons, A. B. "Cultivating the Capacity for Formal Reasoning: Objectives and Procedures in an Introductory Physical Science Course." *American Journal of Physics,* 1976, *44* (9), 834–838.

Champagne, A. B., Klopfer, L. E., and Anderson, J. H. "Factors Influencing the Learning of Classical Mechanics." *American Journal of Physics,* 1980, *48* (12), 1074–1079.

Clement, J. "Students' Preconceptions in Introductory Mechanics." *American Journal of Physics,* 1982, *50* (1), 66–71.

Fuller, R. G. "Solving Physics Problems — How Do We Do It?" *Physics Today,* 1982, *35* (9), 43–47.

Fuller, R. G., Karplus, R., and Lawson, A. E. "Can Physics Develop Reasoning?" *Physics Today,* 1977, *30* (2), 23–28.

Griffiths, D. H. "Physics Teaching: Does It Hinder Intellectual Development?" *American Journal of Physics,* 1976, *44* (1), 81–85.

Lawson, A. E., and Renner, J. W. "Relationships of Science Subject Matter and Developmental Levels of Learners." *Journal of Research in Science Teaching,* 1975, *12* (4), 347–358.

McDermott, L. C., Piternick, L. K., and Rosenquist, M. L. "Helping Minority Students Succeed in Science." *Journal of College Science Teaching* (Parts I, II, and III), 1980, *9* (1, 3, 5), 135–140, 201–205, 261–265.

McKinnon, J. W., and Renner, J. W. "Are Colleges Concerned with Intellectual Development?" *American Journal of Physics,* 1971, *39* (9), 1047–1052.

Reif, F., Larkin, J. H., and Brackett, G. C. "Teaching General Learning and Problem Solving Skills." *American Journal of Physics,* 1976, *44* (3), 212–217.

Rigden, J. S. "Editorial: Both Necessary, Neither Sufficient." *American Journal of Physics,* 1981, *49* (10), 909.

Trowbridge, D. E., and McDermott, L. C. "Investigation of Student Understanding of the Concept of Velocity in One Dimension." *American Journal of Physics,* 1980, *48* (12), 1020–1028.

Trowbridge, D. E., and McDermott, L. C. "Investigation of Student Understanding of the Concept of Acceleration in One Dimension." *American Journal of Physics,* 1981, *49* (3), 242–253.

Wadsworth, B. J. *Piaget for the Classroom Teacher.* New York: Longman, 1978.

Beverly A. P. Taylor is an assistant professor of physics at Jackson State University. She received her Ph.D. in physics from Clemson University in 1978. The work described in this chapter was begun during the academic year 1980–81, when she was a Lilly Foundation postdoctoral teaching fellow.

Teaching the sociology of mental health and illness can be greatly improved and enriched through a multidisciplinary course that includes views of madness presented in works of fiction, drama, poetry, music, art, and also through studying the opinions and attitudes of various elements of society.

Teaching a Multidisciplinary Course on Mental Illness

Phil Brown

In 1981 I was invited to be a postdoctoral teaching fellow as part of Brown University's Lilly Endowment–funded program. My participation in the program gave me the opportunity to design a new course that met my department's curricular needs and student needs and that also gave me a chance to extend my own scope as a teacher and as a psychiatric sociologist. I chose to develop a course titled "The Many Perceptions of Mental Illness."

"The Many Perceptions of Mental Illness" stemmed from my effort to expand the limits of a course I already taught, "The Sociology of Mental Health and Illness." This type of course, offered in a large number of sociology departments, examines the extent of mental illness in society; public attitudes toward mental illness; psychiatric institutions' ideology, structure, and practices; public mental health policy; the training, beliefs, and practices of mental health professionals; and the ways in which mental illness is a major aspect of deviant behavior. Such expansion involved exploring the social and cultural context that could enrich the standard course of its type.

In itself, I thought this would be a useful project, although I already believed I had accomplished this enrichment to a significant

P. A. Lacey (Ed.). *Revitalizing Teaching Through Faculty Development.* New Directions for Teaching and Learning, no. 15. San Francisco: Jossey-Bass, September 1983.

degree — even to the point of including fiction, drama, and poetry in the course that I had taught many times before coming to Brown. On reflection, however, I realized I had only used literature to illustrate sociological concepts. For example, Chekhov's *Ward Number Six* was a good explication of psychiatry's diagnostic bias and professionalism. Also, mental patients' poetry was useful in pointing out personal anguish and institutional constraints. But I became convinced that the ubiquity of mental illness and its social significance required more than mere illustration; it necessitated exploring the differing perceptions and world views held by different groups toward the multifaceted phenomenon broadly termed *mental illness*. I needed to devise ways to see literature and the arts as modes of perception and expression, both regarding mental illness and about being mentally ill. I wanted to show students how this social phenomenon reverberated so differently in various people's lives. Thus I wrote in my course description for the catalogue:

> Mental illness has figured largely in poetry, fiction, the arts, and music. Many of the perceptions of mental illness form key parts of childhood socialization and adult belief systems. The mad artist, the frightening asylum, the mentally ill relative in the family closet, fear of a halfway house in the neighborhood, the mental patients' terror and desolation — all these are part of the many perceptions of mental illness.

Essential to this approach was an attempt to involve students in deeper discussions and to tap their affective involvement in the topic. But an incident from a past course shows how such involvement is difficult to evoke. My favorite undergraduate courses had long been about my two specialty areas: "Medical Sociology" and "Sociology of Mental Health and Illness." In teaching the former, I always obtained a large amount of student participation; since everyone has had some involvement in the health care system, students easily contributed insights based on their own experience or the experience of those close to them. But in the mental health course such participation was rarely forthcoming. Once, in a small class of about fifteen students, one person added to a discussion point by remarking on her experience in psychotherapy. It was a valuable comment, and not at all what might be called too personal or self-involved. Yet, except for the student's friend, no one was able to respond to the sharing of the personal experience.

The statistics of mental illness and of minor emotional problems, such as the kind described by my student, tell us that several students in the class must have had some involvement in the mental health care system, either directly or through family or friends. Why could they not draw on their own experiences in class discussion? Why could they not respond when one student did speak out of experience? Stigma alone could not be the answer, since in other courses my students volunteered information on petty crime and drug and alcohol abuse, which are also stigmatized subjects. I believe the answer was that despite the wide prevalence of mental illness, students had few skills for or practice in discussing it themselves. Most people fear that only professionals are capable of dealing with emotional disturbance. Also, the sociological material of the course may have created an academic barrier between the subject matter and the actual pervasiveness of mental illness, which made it a difficult topic for emotionally involved discussion.

My project was to present this pervasiveness vividly — to show how so many of our daily cultural and institutional frameworks are touched by madness, by the fear of madness, and even by the fear of dealing with the normal emotional components of daily life. Students needed to learn about the degree to which our culture conditions us to either ignore emotional life or to treat it in an entertaining fashion (for example, the instant intimacy of the pop "therapies" such as "I'm OK, You're OK" and encounter groups). Students would then hopefully understand that fear of, or inexperience in, examining emotional life contributes to the general fear and stigma surrounding madness. Definitions of insanity also reflect many of our definitions of normality and our experience of the human condition. Therefore, I wanted the course to have a broad, humanistic application in its exploration of how normality is defined. Students could learn that the development of their own and other societies includes the development of a set of attitudes toward the limits of the human mind, even in a breakdown state. This aspect of the course would ultimately involve general social theory, which is itself multidisciplinary, and would therefore necessitate breaking down the fragmentary boundaries between disciplines that so often plague the mental health field.

My sociological goals in this course included demonstrating that the many perceptions of mental illness that are covered become understandable within the framework of sociological analysis. Sociology has played a major role in health and mental health care, offering assistance in many areas of theory, research, and clinical/social practice. More than psychology, psychiatry, or social work, sociology has provided a broad, comprehensive view of mental health and illness. There is sociological material in one of the course's major sections. And, in fact, student comments led me to present the sociological material at the beginning of the semester rather than toward the end, so that this orientation would inform the other course material.

I wanted students to leave the course with a sociological understanding of mental illness. However, this is different from a more detailed and applied learning that students would get in the usual sociology course on mental health or illness. In those classes, they leave with a knowledge of incidence and prevalence rates, third-party reimbursement practices, race and gender differences in diagnosis and treatment, and NIMH policy making. But I was after something else, although sociology would still remain the key point for the course.

Structure of "The Many Perceptions of Mental Illness"

I organized the course in four main sections. First, I wanted to show mental illness as a central aspect of social life. This would perform several functions: change some student anxieties about madness and mad people, increase awareness of what constitutes madness in this society, and persuade students that they really could learn about life by studying mental illness. Second, I wanted to show examples of mental illness as expressed in the arts, since these are both repositories of our cultural structure as well as vivid, emotional manifestations of madness. Students could then learn that some people are "mad" only in that they respond to the insane elements of their world, while for others mental illness may create a marvelous artistic product that sensitizes both the sane and the insane to a deeper appreciation of life. Third, I turned to sociological critiques and approaches to mental illness. This focuses the material and introduces a general perspective that replaces the scattered perceptions learned so far. In the fourth and final section, students see examples of the mental health system in practice through guest speakers who describe local facilities and agencies. A more detailed discussion of each section and the course's general progress follows.

Section One: Mental Illness as a Central Aspect of Social Life. My opening lecture addresses the many facets of human existence that are touched by madness, as well as the fear of madness in society and the definition of madness in general. This lecture is accompanied by students reading Ken Kesey's well-known personal indictment of mental hospitals, *One Flew Over the Cuckoo's Nest,* and a viewing of Frederick Wiseman's "Titticut Follies," a *cinéma vérité* look at the dehumanization of patients in Massachusetts' Bridgewater State Hospital for the Criminally Insane. I also provide handouts to illustrate the widespread application of psychiatric stigma, such as a muffler store's advertisement of shock absorbers with bold print headlines reading "Shock Therapy." This opening overview is followed by R. D. Laing's *The Divided Self* to present the existential-phenomenological clinical view of madness. Laing's work is valuable for its clinical accuracy, its sympathetic involvement with the patient's world view and suffering, its critique of traditional psychiatry, and its use of creative prose to convey case histories — a tradition Laing inherited from Ludwig Binswanger (students also read a brief excerpt from his work).

The first assignment, a two- to four-page informal statement of the student's initial perceptions of mental illness upon beginning the course, is due at the start of the week on Laingian approaches. The paper gives students a chance to briefly explore their attitudes toward mental illness and gives me a glimpse of the variety of approaches they have to the subject. Also, it prepares students for the final assignment at the end of the semester, a five- to seven-page review and re-evaluation of their initial perceptions. Students hand in this last paper along with the first paper (including my comments), thus providing me with a map of the course's impact on each individual.

Section Two: Mental Illness in the Arts. In the first week of this section, students read first-person accounts of going mad or being mad: Sylvia Plath's short story "Johnny Panic and the Bible of Dreams" and Barbara Gordon's popular novel of Valium withdrawal–induced psychosis, *I'm Dancing as Fast as I Can.* Next we explore some social contexts of madness by reading Charlotte Perkins Gilman's *The Yellow Wallpaper* and Marge Piercy's *Woman on the Edge of Time.* Both are feminist approaches to insanity, in which biases within the psychiatric profession and patriarchal definitions of mental illness are addressed. A lecture by a psychiatrist/psychoanalyst from the medical school faculty offers another view of these approaches. He argues against the general social-context positions of Gordon and Piercy and what he considers the naive approaches of Laing and of Peter Shaffer (whose play *Equus* is the next topic). The psychiatrist believes that the characters of Gordon and Piercy reflect actual paranoia: They manifest fear and anxiety well out of proportion to reality, and they project their personal psychopathology onto the structures of social injustice. He also considers Laing and Schaffer to be glorifiers of madness without adequate regard for actual suffering. The guest lecturer compels the students to grapple with the disparity of viewpoints concerning social structure and mental illness.

Madness as portrayed in dramatic works follows, with Schaffer's *Equus* and Tennessee Williams' *Suddenly Last Summer* as assigned readings. We explore the fallibility and self-doubt of Schaffer's psychiatrist as he confronts his role as "normalizer" of a lifestyle he has found to be unhealthy for the human psyche, including his own. While Schaffer's psychotically violent patient is clearly suffering, we are able to view his illness as part of a pathological family constellation. Similarly, Williams' play shows us the schizophrenogenic family, in which the patient's apparent mental illness is due to an entire family's unlabelled madness. While reading the literary works, the students begin work on a writing assignment. Each student writes a seven- to ten-page paper that examines one work of their own choosing from a long list I provide of fiction, drama, and memoirs of mental illness in light of class lectures and discussions of the literary treatment of mental illness. The assignment sheet asks students to consider ways in which literature and art have been analyzed in class:

> For instance, is mental illness the primary theme in the work, or is it just a small part? Is the mentally ill character considered deviant, evil, or threatening? Is insanity used as a general social theme? Is insanity realistically portrayed? Is it affectively (emotionally) powerful? Does it increase your understanding and experience of madness?

This paper is due at the end of the section on the arts.

The theme of madness in music focuses on rock and pop music that deals directly with such experiences. My audio tape features the Jefferson Airplane's "Lather," the Rolling Stones' "19th Nervous Breakdown" and "Mother's Little Helper," Pink Floyd's "Brain Damage," Joni Mitchell's version of "Twisted," and Supertramp's "Asylum." I provide introductions and commentary on the songs and use them to demonstrate how widespread the portrayal of insanity is in popular music. Were there more time, I might add material on portrayals of madness in classical music, such as operatic "mad scenes."

I include three slide presentations of representations of madness in art in the second section. The first is on Van Gogh, presented by an art historian and museum curator from a nearby college. Works by Van Gogh shown in the slide show include "Starry Night," "Self-Portrait," "Crows over the Wheatfield," and "Shoes." Van Gogh is described as the prototypical mad artist, and this guest lecturer talks about how different people have viewed the artist's emotional state and introduces students to the widespread notion of the mad artist in general. Next I do a slide presentation on other mad artists and on portrayals of madness by artists not considered mentally ill. I include Goya (for example, "The Madhouse at Saragossa," "Procession of the Flagellants," and

"Here Comes the Bogey-Man"), Bosch ("Ship of Fools" and "Tree Man"), and Breughel ("Mad Meg"). These artists maintain their sanity while at the same time they portray the limits of sanity and the madness of the world. William Blake's work portrays some similar themes, but loses its sane "edge" at times as he delves into a fantasy world, as seen in "Los," "Nebuchadnezzar," and "The Number of the Beast." Albrecht Durer's "Melancholia" and Gericault's "The Mad Assassin" portray madness with clinically useful detail. Edvard Munch ("The Scream," "The Red Vine," and "Angst") and James Ensor ("Skeleton Studying Chin," "Demons Pursuing Me," and "Self-Portrait with Demons") are well-known artists who suffered emotional breakdowns that they were able to portray in their work.

My hope is that students will enrich themselves with the tools of perception offered by these artists. Artistic perception here includes many different explorations of the unconscious mind and of the conscious emotional life, including visions of alternative societies (for example Blake). In discussing madness and the visual arts, students confront the problem of why such moving expressions of psychological processes often are located at, or beyond, the limits of sanity. My third slide presentation focuses on the artwork of mental patients, done both for artistic release and art therapy. This show provides an important glimpse into patients' self-concepts and personal suffering, as well as a look at the utility of art in diagnosis and therapy. I also point out the connections between "psychotic art" and "established art."

Section Three: Sociological Critiques. I spend one week of the course on the sociological critique of the medical model and one on the social structure of the mental hospital. The critique of the medical model examines the flaws in the unidimensional psychiatric and psychological models that see mental illness as a mechanical process without sufficient attention paid to patients' social contexts. A medical model stresses very specific interventions at the individual or, at best, family levels, rather than understanding of the broader structural fabric that determines individual and group development. Medical models include biochemical, psychoanalytic, or behavioristic analyses of mental illness. Material for this area includes experimental demonstrations of diagnostic bias and inaccuracy, clinical studies, sociological critiques, and short stories by Frigyes Karinthy ("Psychiatry") and Allan Wheelis ("The League of Death"). The topic on social structure of the mental hospital employs Erving Goffman's classic study, *Asylums,* as well as fiction — Poe's short story, "The System of Dr. Tarr and Professor Fether," and Chekhov's short novel, *Ward Number Six.* By combining fiction with social science in these topics, I can draw connections with the prior section on madness in the arts and demonstrate the various perspectives that can be brought to bear on the study of social institutions. I also show the documentary, "Hurry Tomorrow," for a critical look at a California State Hospital.

Next, we explore the often conflicting worldviews and attitudes of different groups and institutions involved in the mental health system. The first of these topics, "Mental Illness from the Patient's Point of View," includes Hannah Greene's classic, *I Never Promised You a Rose Garden,* a marvelous experiential account that includes both a patient's suffering and her later outlook as a therapist. Other selections include writings of expatients angered by the treatment they received. Some remain antagonistic to psychiatry and others, like Clifford Beers (founder of the American Foundation for Mental Hygiene in 1928), have joined with concerned psychiatrists to foster public education about, and involvement in, mental care. Students learn about the mental patients' rights movement during the following week by reading my own research and Judi Chamberlin's *On Our Own: Patient-Controlled Alternatives to the Mental Health System.* Chamberlin herself comes to class as a guest speaker to present her controversial point of view. At this point, another seven-to-ten page paper is due, examining the various patient perspectives and the sociological approaches. This assignment compels students to evaluate the legitimacy of patients' angry responses and sociologists' critical research, which is difficult for many of them — especially the psychology majors and pre-med students — since they usually cannot accept such vehement criticism of the medical model.

Section Four: Public Attitudes Toward Madness. In the final section, we examine public attitudes by studying the portrayal of mental illness in the mass media and by hearing several guest speakers — the director of the state's Mental Health Association and two graduate students from the American Civilization program at Brown, who conducted oral history and document research into public advocacy for improved mental illness and retardation policies in the state. As a sequel, students read articles by supporters and opponents of residential treatment facilities in communities and hear a guest lecture by the director of a local nonprofit organization that operates several group homes. (An attempt to locate a guest speaker from a group opposing neighborhood facilities was unsuccessful.) During this week, each section of approximately twenty students role-plays a typical situation involving neighborhood opposition to a community home for the mentally ill, based on a handout that describes a basic scenario and provides a roster of actors. Students are allowed some time to prepare, but improvisation in the role-playing is emphasized. Time is reserved so that each section has the opportunity to review their recently completed dramatization. Students are asked how authentic their role-playing was, and frequently they find themselves expressing their actual beliefs. Role-playing and the review that follows is invaluable in demonstrating the unconscious and semiconscious levels of social attitudes toward mental illness.

Students finish up the course by reading labor union and National Institute of Mental Health perspectives on mental health policy. The director of a large community mental health center and an official of the aides' union local at the state's mental hospital also give presentations. On the final day of class we have a summing-up discussion and students hand in their final papers.

Impact of the Course

I soon found that students had different expectations for the course. Pre-med students and some psychology majors balked at criticism of the mental health system, while sociology, health and society, and other psychology students did not. This particular tension was very useful. It prompted purposeful argument and highlighted the actual power struggles underway in the mental health field. Of course, not every student can be completely satisfied by a course with such a varied focus. For example, some students wanted more clinical reading material and those who were literature majors wanted more in-depth literary criticism of the work. But, despite different expectations, students were exceptionally involved in classroom discussion, weekly session meetings, and assignments. The films and guest speakers sparked further interest, and the participatory assignments such as poetry readings and the role-playing described earlier were particularly successful. I had a larger than usual number of students visit my office, another sign of interest. Four students came to me the next semester requesting to be undergraduate teaching assistants, even without pay, so that they could further pursue the course material.

I believe my excitement in creating the course was conveyed in the classroom. I learned a great deal in the process about content, teaching methods, and sources of materials. The course enriched my research, including my book on mental hospital policy and a companion anthology. It aided my research on mental hospital staff attitudes toward patients' rights and led to a conference paper on the right to refuse treatment, as well as an article on mental patients as victims and victimizers for a colleague's criminology collection. Reading to prepare lectures and to expand my knowledge of new areas reminded me of the importance of a multidisciplinary approach to mental health care, which psychiatric sociology sometimes ignores.

At times I was convinced that my lack of expertise in the arts — particularly in the visual arts — would hamper my application of this material. Colleagues in those areas were helpful, and I did a good deal of background work in the library. But I do feel that this area of the course can use more development. At times I had to remind myself that I was not expected to be an expert in each separate area; my goal was to be an expert in tying together the various areas.

The Lilly Teaching Fellows Program, in tandem with Brown University's summer support preceding it, provided an excellent forum for improving my teaching skills. Teaching goals and methods were discussed at two Lilly conferences, with Lilly staff members, with other Lilly fellows and related program participants at Brown, with other Brown faculty in and outside of my department, and with a number of external resource people. There was a jumping-off point for extensive teaching discussions, something that unfortunately is not built into our academic lives. I discovered a wide assortment of individuals who were eager to discuss this course and more general teaching issues. They included literature and art professors, an art museum curator, the director of the art department's slide room, the curator of a poetry collection in the Brown library system, an art slide photographer, and staff members of public and private mental health agencies and organizations.

Therefore, I now have a deeper appreciation for the challenges of multidisciplinary and creative teaching. The Lilly program provided a fine framework within which I could exercise my own interests in teaching. But other conditions are necessary for such innovative programs to succeed. Scholars must see a way to link pedagogical experimentation with the research programs they feel required to carry out for job security (here I am clearly speaking to junior faculty, who make up the bulk of Lilly fellows), and time and resources are mandatory. I could not have done the job I did without summer support, a half-time (one course) teaching reduction in the preceding term, and funds for films, speakers, art slides, and an undergraduate teaching assistant who joined the regular graduate student TA's in order to provide smaller than usual discussion sections. The self-directed meetings on campus of Lilly fellows also provided the climate of encouragement and support that I needed.

Most importantly, during the summer and fall semester before my course, and during the spring semester when I taught the course, I was more immersed in "The Many Perceptions of Mental Illness" than in any undergraduate course I had ever prepared. This level of involvement cannot be replicated yearly, although I can apply lessons derived from my experience in less intense efforts. In general, I believe my students learned that mental health and illness must be seen in a large, complex social context, that madness reverberates throughout much of our lives, and that we can learn much about ourselves and our "normal" world through such study.

*Phil Brown is assistant professor of sociology at Brown
University, where he teaches medical sociology, sociology
of mental health and illness, and social welfare policy. His
research on mental health policy and mental patients' rights
has appeared in the* Journal of Community Psychology,
International Journal of Health Services, Mental Disability
Law Reporter, *and* Social Science & Medicine.
He is currently at work on a book, The Transfer of Care:
Psychiatric Deinstitutionalization and Its Aftermath,
and is editing a volume, Mental Health Care and Social
Policy *(both to be published by Routledge & Kegan Paul).
His current research concerns hospital staff attitudes toward
mental patients' rights.*

*An introductory literature course should introduce students
to more than a body of material and a range of techniques
and traditions. It should teach literary interpretation as
a process of inquiry useful in other situations in which we
shape the world through language.*

Fiction and Fact: On Trial

Jean Ferguson Carr

Any introductory course proposes a value and terrain for its discipline
and claims a way for beginners to enter the world of the expert. Whether
or not such claims are publicly articulated as course goals, teachers of
such courses present certain attitudes and material as "basic" to their
field's methods and discourse. Many beginning courses are designed to
introduce students, both prospective majors and the general student
alike, to the most professional aspects of the field, treating all students
as apprentice biologists, psychologists, or designers. However, introductory courses in literature have traditionally stressed general humanistic education, taking on the responsibility for an introduction to culture, morals, ethics, and good taste. Benjamin DeMott argued in 1970
that the "right" English course is one "that prizes the poem and the play
as windows opening on a livingness that would otherwise be unseen
and dead to the human eye" (p. 159). A decade later the Commission on
the Humanities (1980) made a similar claim: "Literature broadens personal moral vision through exploring character, circumstance, and
choice" (pp. 69–70). In a curiously noncommittal discussion, the Commission praised the humanities for such vague qualities as their "inti-

I would like to thank the Lilly Endowment for a postdoctoral teaching award
fellowship in 1980–81 to work on this course and other curricular projects. I would also
like to acknowledge my debts to colleagues Ann Hayes, John Hart, and Lynne Barrett,
with whom I initiated the course, and to Peggy Knapp and Paul Kameen, who shared
in its development.

P. A. Lacey (Ed.). *Revitalizing Teaching Through Faculty Development.* New Directions
for Teaching and Learning, no. 15. San Francisco: Jossey-Bass, September 1983.

mate connections with ideas." And perhaps in an effort to justify the humanities in a climate of preprofessional education, the report stressed how the study of humanities and literature would aid students in acquiring important skills in critical analysis and reading. Such defenses skirt our current unsettled sense of the value and role of literature in education and show how difficult it is to define the aims of an introduction to the field.

Generalized claims about the humanistic value of such courses do not provide a very strong rationale in the 1980s, when professional training seems almost mandatory and when humanism is under political attack. I want to describe some of the problems facing teachers of introductory literature courses and to discuss a course called *Fiction and Fact,* designed as the literature course in Carnegie-Mellon University's core curriculum. In defending its inclusion in a strongly professional and skills-oriented curriculum, I had to develop clearly articulated claims about the value and nature of humanistic skills or attitudes, about what it means to be a literary expert, and about how such expertise is useful to people who will not continue as literature majors. In the process of designing the course, I think I developed a much more rigorous sense of what literary professionals think important and useful about the ways of perceiving and interpreting the world that their discipline encourages.

Anyone who designs an introductory course faces the multiple preconceptions of the students, who may regard literary texts and study as escapist and irrelevant or obscure and overly refined. Collins (1980) notes that students who do not already understand and accept the value of literary study may be put off or bewildered by a course that assumes as unquestionable precondition the pleasure, significance, and centrality of literature to education. Even students who do accept and delight in reading may see such delight as limited to English class, and experience personally rewarding but with little power to influence their thinking or activities in other fields. Their conclusions may in fact be an accurate reflection of their teachers' own isolation and sense of powerlessness in a university community.

In most colleges today the introductory course has the double function of preparing future English majors for further study in the discipline and of providing those nonmajors—the preprofessional, fine arts, and engineering students—with their one dose of what literature offers. The diversity of our introductory courses shows the strain. We do not rest secure in a clear-cut title, method, or material; we have no "Calculus I and II," no "Beginning Accounting," no "Fundamentals of Design." We do not present well-argued claims about how a student moves from a beginning to intermediate or advanced level; we cannot agree, except in our most defensive posture, on a limited body of knowledge or material to cover. We vaguely claim that reading widely is useful and that some students are more mature readers than others, but it is unclear whether sophistication comes because a student has learned a method for reading new texts or has learned what to say about certain traditions and masterworks. Introductory courses often seem to be the last remnant of an old curriculum, of other days when students invariably took more than one course in the humanities. Survey introductions imply that students will return for in-depth, follow-up courses to fill in the historical continuum of literature. Generic courses stress our professional interest in creating and elaborating literature within categories, and function best if students read more novels, poems, or tragedies after discovering the borders of the genre. Thematic and interdisciplinary courses reveal our concern about showing literature's relevance to significant issues or topics and its usefulness in more marketable fields, but they do not always make clear the rationale for treating literature as something more significant than an example.

Fiction and Fact

The approach to teaching literature I propose shares many of the interests that guide these more traditional introductory approaches. It encourages students to see literary texts as influenced by and influential in their historical contexts. It offers a range of different kinds of fiction, from different periods, countries, and traditions. It organizes its material through a thematic focus on exploring interdisciplinary relations with more fact-oriented disciplines. This course stresses the epistemological relationships among disciplines, rather than focusing primarily on their separate materials or territories. Its theme is that of questioning how we evaluate and label the structures and materials of our world — our "fictions" and "facts." The approach questions how we know and communicate knowledge, that is, how our various disciplinary approaches and allegiances influence our inquiries and our results, a theoretical position informed by Foucault's (1977) sensitivity about the relation of a formal discipline to its "knowledge." It thus stresses the process by which we come to read and revise our worlds, emphasizing a character's (or a reader's) choices and strategies for perceiving, responding to, altering, and constructing his environment.

This approach stresses the usefulness of literary strategies in other intellectual and practical situations by presenting literature both as a process of inquiry and as a powerful, though temporary, image arising from the particular voice, vision of coherence, and intelligence of its creator. We have organized the course's seven book-length narratives into units that focus on (1) the construction and destruction of assumptions through the characters' experience with a strange or mythic world, (2) the creation and interpretation of accustomed or realistic worlds, and (3) the conflicts between personal and social fictions and facts. We thus try to exploit, as Kaufmann has also urged (1977), literature's dialectical relationship with whatever we might term the real world. Literature offers a constructed version of a world through which we can inspect what we think of as "real"; at the same time, the myths, patterns, and metaphors of literature provide us with ways of structuring and communicating our own experiences.

As the title suggests, the course is designed to explore the relationship between what we call fiction and what we call fact, which may initially seem a simple and clear distinction. A beginning assumption may be that fictions are subjective inventions of fantastic worlds to which we can escape for pleasure, for entertainment, or for relief from boredom, and facts are those testable, verifiable, irrevocable entities that constitute and limit our everyday lives. Yet almost any example of multiple perspective suggests that "facts" alter under pressure, under the changed framework of a different time, place, cultural definition, philosophic system, or scientific paradigm. The data that prove one man an effective politician may be used by his opponent to prove him corrupt. The narrative of events offered by one country may completely counter that of a rival nation.

In *Fiction and Fact* we investigate the relationship between literary fictions and other modes of explaining or ordering perceptions—modes that may initially appear to present "the truth" or "reality." We consider, for example, the "literary choices" made in historical narrative in any attribution of cause and effect, as White demonstrates in *Metahistory* (1973). We analyze the metaphors with which scientific, sociological, or political writing persuades us of its authority. Studying literature encourages us to test and challenge the images we rely on in our private and public lives and to be aware of how language shapes our viewpoints. We begin the course, for example, by discussing the language categories by which we judge fictions and facts, by considering such relationships as the linking of the term *real* to concepts of ownership and possession, as in *real estate*. Or we may argue about the changing authority for a universal truth, like the inappropriateness of "Man is the measure of all things" in an age of feminist or environmental awareness. We may discuss the agreements about symbolic communication that allow us to ascribe meaning to "2 + 2 = 4," or we may discuss the shared understanding of metaphoric language that lets us read, without balking, a commonplace like "time stood still," "electrons are particles," or "life is short." In our daily life we may treat such non-literary images as givens and as factual or authoritative. Recognizing their metaphoric nature enables us to be aware of them when such scrutiny is important, as when we need to argue for a change in those metaphors.

Strange and Mythic Worlds

In the first unit in the course we read three texts that offer such competing fictions and emphasize the differing interpretations of evidence that arise from changes in culture, time, place, or person. In this unit to date we have read such texts as Twain's *A Connecticut Yankee in King Arthur's Court,* Ursula LeGuin's *The Left Hand of Darkness,* a pairing of *Beowulf* and John Gardner's *Grendel,* Swift's *Gulliver's Travels,* and Kafka's "The Metamorphosis." All of these books place us in a strange world—either of the past, the future, or of fantasy; they challenge, through a world constructed by the writer, the assumptions and facts we think of as natural or given.

The pairing of *Beowulf* and *Grendel,* for example, invites readers to consider the same events or facts from two radically different perspectives: the eighth century's struggle between heroic and Christian values and the alienated, "monstrous" perspective afforded by twentieth-century doubts. Through Grendel's knowing, cynical eyes, the heroic and religious values of the eighth century seem a tawdry sham that the monster must destroy. Through Beowulf's powerful, insistent eyes, Grendel's cynicism seems lonely and defeatist—the very quality that puts him "monstrously" apart from society's myths and shared constructs. The modern novel opens up the eighth-century myth, encouraging readers to see the supernatural conflicts as mythic commentary on historical problems and the limitations of a world based on violent reprisal and betrayal—a world that lacks enduring traditions of order, governance, or moral rule.

. An encounter between different cultural perspectives is central to Twain's *A Connecticut Yankee in King Arthur's Court.* Hank Morgan, a nineteenth-century technologist who is brashly comfortable about the rightness of his Yankee values, finds himself dislocated, physically and ideologically, when he is thrust back in time to the sixth-century world of King Arthur. Similarly, in LeGuin's *The Left Hand of Darkness,* the envoy from Terra, Genly Ai, must maneuver between two strange cultures on the wintry planet of Karhide. In both books outsiders must learn to examine their own cultural assumptions, seeing the world through strange eyes, and must try to communicate across significant cultural gaps. Both books explore the extreme difficulty of judging even the simplest facts in a foreign context, and they offer an extended metaphor of the problems of reading a strange world or text.

One project we use in this unit is a comparison of three versions of the myth of King Arthur's death. We consider the different cultural values suggested by the strategic choices of which "facts" to present by the three authors: Malory's despair about human failing in *Morte d'Arthur,* Tennyson's concern about losing one's vision of the future in *Idylls of the King,* and T. H. White's earnest longing for a problem-solving, reasonable universe in *The Once and Future King.* The project effectively tests the students' ability to see the difference between the story and the particular telling of a story. Faced with three versions of the same facts, students can move beyond concern about what happens — what the story's "message" or "theme" is — to why it happens that way.

This first unit in *Fiction and Fact* thus explores a sort of relativistic skepticism; it undermines a common assumption that the real world (or any written explanation of it) is finished, stable, absolute — a fact. But this is comparatively easy, since freshmen experience in so many ways during their first year of college the instability of patterns they assumed were universal or natural. It is more difficult to suggest that such relativism is not merely a modern malaise created to unsettle their lives, a blurring of the facts that will go away once we deport all politicians. And it is even more difficult to teach what else literary thinking has to offer: that all language and fiction making can be a way to actively interpret and rebuild some sort of operative certainty about the world and a way to give shared value to our separate experiences. If the first aim of *Fiction and Fact* is to make problematical our assumptions about facts and reality, the second aim is to enable students to have some power over what operates as reality in our world, to construct their own powerful roles and voices, and to take part in the making and interpreting of fictions that influence their lives — intellectually, politically, and personally.

Accustomed Worlds

In the second unit of the course we read about ordinary characters who are engaged in the act of shaping and interpreting the world. Our reading material focuses on how characters negotiate the relationship between their private and public worlds and how they interpret the world they find themselves in by attempting to make it responsive to their needs. In this unit we have read such texts as Cather's *My Antonia*, Solzhenitsyn's *One Day in the Life of Ivan Denisovitch*, Austen's *Pride and Prejudice*, and Zora Neale Hurston's *Their Eyes Were Watching God*. All of these texts are realistic in mode: They present us with characters and situations that seem to reflect our world's operations, even though the time, place, and culture may be as unfamiliar to us as any imagined context. Yet even in these "accustomed worlds" characters must interpret and shape what happens to them. We examine how characters comprehend their situations, their own actions and desires, and those imposed on them by family, friends, or institutions. We examine the various forms of communication—letters, pictures, tales, documents, stories, jokes, and dreams—that ordinary people use to bridge the gaps between their private and public lives.

We also consider how people are governed by various fictions and how their notions of what makes a heroic or full life shape their specific choices. We discuss the helplessness of characters who have no ways of making their lives take shape, of imagining a future, or of communicating a past. For example, in a short class project, we discuss a letter from an immigrant that opens with the claim: "A novel could be made of my life." We ask the students to construct various narratives from the details provided by the writer and to describe the choices and evaluations that an author would have to make to turn the unconnected, unweighted details into a novel. In another writing assignment, students discuss strategies by which characters try to influence the actions and judgments of others and in which characters are actors but also directors and audience for their own scenes. Yet another assignment calls on students to discuss different levels of communication occurring in a scene and to gauge the difference between what is said in formal conversation and what else is conveyed by hints, gestures, dress, physical reactions, and silences. Such approaches invite students to see situations—whether fictional or not—as created and interactive and as a process of communication and response rather than a set enactment of predictable positions. The strategies for reading another person's desires and thoughts—silences as well as speeches—are as useful in students' personal and professional lives as in their literary experiences.

This emphasis on process and interpretation signals a major methodological difference between *Fiction and Fact* and many other introductory literature courses. Instead of presenting literary texts as finished, ordered, artistic products that construct a world that appears seamlessly whole, we stress the discontinuous gaps in the articulated surface—those interpretive problems that make a literary text, like any other text or situation, rhetorical in nature. We stress what Topf praised as a major "skill" that literature can teach: how to deal with "open-endedness, unpredictability, and capacity for conflict" (1981, p. 470).

Worlds on Trial

In the final unit of our course we read texts that place characters' and readers' worlds on trial. We have assigned Dickens's *Great Expectations* or *Bleak House*, E. L. Doctorow's *The Book of Daniel*, Stoppard's play *Rosencrantz and Guildenstern Are Dead*, and Kafka's *The Trial*. To emphasize that such shaping and fictionalizing is common to all human situations, not just to those termed literary, we incorporate some nonfictional documents and discuss how they use "fictional" strategies and how they might be reshaped to give different weight or significance to their materials. We have devised group projects on documentary material of the French Revolutionary period (the *cahiers de doléance*, or "notebooks of grievances") and on first-person oral histories from Henry Mayhew's 1851 social survey *London Labour and the London Poor*. In both fiction and nonfiction, relatively ordinary people must be able to interpret and revise their world or situations if they are to survive. The books studied in this unit insist on the importance of being able to read, write, and speak in and about your world in order to avoid becoming someone else's or an institution's object, statistic, or victim. Each book or set of documents posits a central relationship between the written word — whether it be a constitution, the Law, chance, or history — and characters' everyday activities and understanding.

An assignment that effectively demonstrates how important it is for individuals to shape the evidence of their experience and to be able to convey those experiences persuasively to an indifferent, if not hostile audience, is the discussion of three *cahiers de doléance*. The *cahiers* were prepared by every rank of French society for consideration by the King shortly before the French Revolution. Interpretation of their experiences was essential for the French peasants, who were being asked to explain their world, to evaluate its limitations and evils, and to propose changes that would make it liveable. Their only hope was to construct a fiction powerful enough to undermine the fictions that oppressed them. The *cahiers* reveal the power of larger, shaping visions: The simplest of them offers a list of unweighted, unevaluated grievances, whereas the most sophisticated shows how one wrong leads to another or how one physical wrong exemplifies a less visible but more significant political evil.

Similar attempts to construct a new world through writing and metaphoric power can be seen in the novels by Dickens or Doctorow, in which characters and narrators must sift through masses of details and possible clues to propose some solution to the chaos. The readings stress the personal danger that results when people cannot articulate the grievances they feel — whether personal, social, judicial, or familial. The novels also stress the imaginative power necessary merely to survey the evidence of an individual case or of one brought against society, much less to resolve it in any reasonable, orderly fashion. The interpretive strategies for reading long and complicated narratives reflect these internal issues. Although a novel like *Bleak House* seems a staggering assignment for a freshman course, by the time they reach this unit students have developed methods for suspending judgment and for juggling multiple constraints and details without insisting on premature closure.

Our final text, Kafka's *The Trial,* offers an extremely powerful experience in interpreting a hostile or unfamiliar world. *The Trial* alters one feature of what we think our world is: It upsets what we think of as the world's logic and asks us to imagine functioning without it. As such, it puts on trial our own ways of understanding and gives us the controlled opportunity to try other ways. K's trial functions both as his judgment and as his punishment. It reveals the inadequacies of his society as he has understood it, and it also can be seen as a trial of his ability to understand, to ask questions, to hear answers, and to sift out clues or to get people to help him. The book enacts the process of reading and fiction making we develop in the course as a whole, stressing the need to imagine new situations and to attend to details that may not suit our preconceptions. We can argue about the other choices K might have made at every stage and about the other interpretations possible, given the evidence. We share K's limited perspective, but we need not share his limited repertoire of interpretive strategies.

"Fiction" and "Fact" Revisited

In the course I have described we try to teach students, through the study of literature, how to question the fictions and facts we read and live by. Such an approach to reading is extremely useful as well in teaching students to write. They learn to write interpretive, evaluative, questioning papers that reflect a self-awareness about strategies for ordering and critiquing. And it is useful in teaching them to discuss — to weigh and value perspectives not their own — and to communicate their own assumptions and conclusions persuasively. Issues of how the questioner shapes his responses, how the empiricist influences his data, and how the clinician invites certain types of answers all show the interdisciplinary, practical value of focusing on how individuals create their world of assumptions and definitions. Our own world, we come to recognize, is made up of interwoven perspectives and fictions in much the same way as the author makes a world for his characters. By studying strange and unfamiliar worlds from characters' points of view, we can begin to distance ourselves from our own culture's perspective to glimpse its architecture, to study its form, and to judge its quality. And we can learn this, not as an abstract generalization but as a constant aspect of our interpretive decisions in the world.

References

Collins, M. J. "The Role of Literature in a College Curriculum." *Liberal Education,* Winter 1980, *66* (4), 382–387.

Commission on the Humanities. *The Humanities in America: Report of the Commission on the Humanities.* Berkeley, Calif.: University of California, 1980.

DeMott, B. "Reading, Writing, Reality, Unreality." In L. S. Josephs and E. R. Steinberg (Eds.), *English Education Today.* New York: Noble and Noble, 1970.

Foucault, M. *Discipline and Punish: The Birth of the Prison* (A. Sheridan, trans.). New York: Pantheon, 1977.

Kaufmann, W. *The Future of the Humanities.* New York: Readers's Digest Press, 1977.

Topf, M. A. "Smooth Things: The Rockefeller Commission's Report on the Humanities." *College English,* 1981, *43* (5), 463–470.

White, H. V. *Metahistory: The Historical Imagination in Nineteenth-Century Europe.* Baltimore: Johns Hopkins University Press, 1973.

Jean Ferguson Carr is an assistant professor of English and director for 1980–1983 of the freshman literature course, Fiction and Fact, *at Carnegie-Mellon University. She is the textual editor of two volumes of* The Collected Works of Ralph Waldo Emerson *(Harvard University Press, 1979, 1983).*

Because college students often lack thinking skills that therefore should be developed, professors must train themselves for this challenge.

Teaching Analytical and Thinking Skills in a Content Course

Curtina Moreland-Young

Students should develop in college the tools that allow them to analyze, synthesize, utilize, internalize, and interpret information. College teaching should be geared toward the further use of these tools. But, too often college students have only reached the early stage of developing these skills, and they are not taught to refine them. Furthermore, few college professors receive any training in teaching. Incorporating teaching and learning procedures that aid in the development of creative and analytical problem-solving skills in students presents a challenge for which many professors are ill prepared. University professors are expected to digest the material of their fields and pay no attention to teaching this knowledge to students, so professors find themselves imitating teachers who probably learned to teach by trial and error. Moreover, the emphasis in most university faculties is on research, not teacher effectiveness. Therefore, the energies of most professors are directed away from classroom performance.

In my twelve years of teaching on the university level, I have seldom observed effective teachers being rewarded or commended, but

P. A. Lacey (Ed.). *Revitalizing Teaching Through Faculty Development.* New Directions for Teaching and Learning, no. 15. San Francisco: Jossey-Bass, September 1983.

I have constantly observed the rewards and commendations meted out for successful proposals and research. Indeed, most of the academicians regarded as being at the pinnacle of their careers are there for reasons other than teaching effectiveness. Even in universities like Jackson State, where teaching effectiveness is rewarded in promotion decisions, teaching may be at odds with research. It seems that we academicians make sharp categorical distinctions between good teachers and good researchers, as if these roles are mutually exclusive. Certainly, anyone who is an effective teacher does research, although a successful researcher is not necessarily an effective teacher. I believe that a good teacher is aware of the newest frontiers in her discipline, is an active researcher, and that this helps to make the classroom environment more exciting.

Before the postdoctoral teaching fellows program began at Jackson State, there were a number of campus resources to aid in stimulating greater teacher efficacy, but they were basically support services and did not provide released time. Although I availed myself of some of these resources, I needed a more systematic method that would stimulate me more than passing reflections about the problems of my students and my teaching effectiveness. During my second year at Jackson State I received information about a new teaching fellowship program that was geared toward addressing a teaching and learning problem and trying to solve it. There might be many by-products of this work, including research and publications, but the main purpose of the released-time grant was to give faculty a chance to become better teachers. I decided to submit a proposal to the program.

I outlined two basic problems in my teaching of political science: Students were not yet able to be either analytical or creative in their thinking about the materials I presented, and I did not know what to do about developing their thinking. Consequently, I proposed a project that would allow me a greater understanding of the learning process and help me to stimulate analytic and creative thinking skills. Since the proposal was funded for the academic year, I decided that the implementation of the project would take place in three phases.

Implementation of the Project

During the first phase of the project, which took place over the fall semester, I was able to reflect on my teaching and to become acquainted with the latest resources available. The search for appropriate teaching strategies revealed a dearth of current literature on teaching analytic and creative thinking skills on the college level in political science. (The journal *Teaching Political Science* is a notable exception.) However, on the elementary and secondary levels of the social sciences, such literature was readily available. I found myself studying teaching models developed by such noted theorists in learning motivation as Jean Piaget, Hilda Taba, and Jerome Bruner. After extensive reading I had a better understanding of the thinking and learning process, if not a clear understanding of how it took place. I developed a working definition of learning, straight from the dictionary: the act of acquiring knowledge and/or skills. I defined thinking as the act of exercising the mind. It also became apparent that I would need to develop some measurement for the key terms *analytical* and *creative* in reference to thinking. I decided that analytic thinking would have taken place if students were able to interpret, evaluate, or apply the information presented to them. Creative thinking would involve new approaches to applying that knowledge. If I were to become effective in teaching creative and analytic thinking skills, I would have to develop techniques that exercised students' minds and required them to engage in drills that moved them toward my ideas about what analytic and creative thinking are.

In the second phase of the project, which started the last part of the first semester and concluded at the end of the second, I applied the ideas I had developed in the first phase of the project. Toward the end of the first semester I met with the project administrator and faculty colleagues who had expertise in my project area. I then tried to restructure course materials and develop exercises that would be used in the course. I knew that if I were successful in this project, I could make creative and analytic thinking exercises a permanent part of the course after its first year and eventually have an impact on future students in the Department of Political Science.

"Introduction to Comparative Politics" was chosen as the experimental course. Although the thinking skills I hoped to develop in the project could be readily used in any course I taught, the comparative class was particularly suited for them, since the content is theoretical and analytical and lends itself to problem solving. In addition, the students who take this course are primarily sophomore political science majors, so I thought the skills they developed would be useful in other courses. From the beginning, I made students aware that they would be involved in an experimental project by explaining it to them and making the course description reflect its importance:

> In addition to the obvious purpose of the course, that of acquiring a body of knowledge about comparative politics, its objective will be to fully develop the creative and analytical thinking skills of the student enrolled in the class. This will be accom-

plished through a series of class exercises, exams, and written assignments.

Course Work

Classroom Exercises. I set aside one class meeting a week to engage in specific exercises designed to stimulate creative and analytic thinking. One such exercise was based on Hilda Taba's learning motivation model and was developed by Dr. Percy Gambrell in the Political Science Department at Jackson State University, who advised me about its use. I modified it for my own purposes.

Students are presented with information that they are asked to interpret. They are asked to look at a piece of data but are not told beforehand what it is. Through a series of questions and answers the students eventually discern that these are drawings of population tables, and then they surmise that the population tables are those of three different countries. At no time during the exercise do I volunteer any information. I only confirm correct statements, being careful to offer positive reinforcements. The following describes a typical exchange:

> *Instructor:* "I am now going to give you some information. You are to look at the information and decide what it is."
> *Student:* "This looks like some kind of table. Is it?"
> *Instructor:* "Yes. Would you explain to the class how you arrived at that conclusion? What kind of table is it?"

After the class agrees that this is a population table of specific countries, I ask them to make statements about these countries using only the information given in the tables. During the exercise I place students in groups, trying to make sure that each group has a mix of strong, weak, and average students. Usually I choose the weak students to be the groups' spokespersons. Placing the students in groups serves three purposes: It makes the exercise more manageable, it gives the weak and moderate students a chance to observe the thought processes of stronger peers within a nonthreatening context, and it helps to build the academic confidence of the weak student by requiring him or her to be the spokesperson. After conferring for five to ten minutes, each group makes its report:

> *Student:* "In looking at the first country, we have decided we can make the following statements. First, there seems to have been a successful birth control program, since there is a low percentage of the population in the 0–4

age bracket compared with women in the population in their fertile years. Second, we think there was a major catastrophe like a plague, but more likely a war, because there is a sharp decline in the age bracket of 25–39. There are fewer people in that age bracket than in the 40–59 bracket."

Instructor: "You've done quite a good job. What projections about the future could you make about the country?"

Student: "There will be a significant pull on the countries' social health services, which address the needs of the elderly."

Instructor: "What information tells you that?"

Student: "The fact that there is a significant population over the age of sixty and that a number of people live over the age of eighty-five. Additionally, we think the country is probably a technologically advanced society because of the low birth rate and long life span of its inhabitants."

Instructor: "Tell me what kind of political situation exists?"

Student: "We don't know. There is no available information."

Instructor: "Good, that's important to realize."

After careful studying, the students were not only able to interpret the information but could also develop plausible theories based on the information gained from their interpretation of the data.

Exams. In order to emphasize the importance of the classroom exercises and to test them as a learning tool, class exams were structured to reflect students' acquisition of knowledge and their ability to attack and solve problems. "Introduction to Comparative Politics" is a course focused on how different comparative scholars approach the analysis of political systems. Some exam questions combined the exercises and course content:

Lucien Pye has developed a model in which he considers the personality factors to be the most important considerations in studying nation building and public administration in developing nations. In his book on Burma, *Politics, Personality, and Nation Building,* he presents his central thesis, summarized as follows:

1. Large, complex, effective and thus flexible organizational forms are a crucial feature of modern society.
2. Large, complex organizations cannot be flexible and effective unless, in addition to their formal struc-

tures, there exist significant informal structures, especially informal channels of communication.
3. Only individuals who have developed associational sentiments can form and effectively participate in these informal structures.
4. Individuals who are insecure and distrustful cannot manifest association sentiments.

Therefore: (Choose/circle the correct choices)

1. Organizations in which a significant proportion of members are insecure and distrustful cannot have effective formal structures.
2. A modern society which by definition has large, complex, effective, and hence flexible organization cannot develop when the crucial large scale organizations have a disproportionate number of insecure and distrustful individuals in them.
3. Individuals can only develop associational sentiments in patriarchal societies.

Research Papers. A natural outgrowth, although not one of my original objectives for the project, was the need to help students develop analytical thinking by writing logically constructed and analytical research papers. Traditionally, students in the "Introduction to Comparative Politics" class are required to select a problem, such as nation building in the Philippines, research it, and then write a major paper. Previously, I was disappointed by the pedestrian nature of many of the papers. I hoped that the exercises conducted in class would have an impact upon the papers produced. I also developed, with the aid of the writing specialist in the University Academic Learning Center, writing exercises to help students improve their own writing in terms of clarity, logic, and continuity of thought. Students were instructed to identify major thesis and topic sentences, transitional sentences, and the conclusion. In class we analyzed selected anonymous student papers using that formula. Their exams and papers were written with more care as a result of this.

Impact of the Course

The third phase of the project was spent in reflection and evaluation. There were basically three positive outgrowths of the project: It increased the self-confidence of the weaker students in class; it provided a challenge to the more adept students, who strove harder to reach their potential; and it helped all students to write exams that were more concise and precise. But, in addition to these positive outcomes, I recognized some structural impediments to the success of my project. Because many students in their precollege years are not encouraged to engage in creative and analytical thinking, they have difficulty learning to do so in college. Often in the precollege years the memorization and regurgitative process, which presumes there is one right answer and an infallible teacher, is fostered. But, to instill creative and analytical thinking skills, the student must learn that she is a reservoir of knowledge. This requires a teacher who is less interested in the right answer and more interested in the thinking process for discovering the right answer. In fact, there may be many right answers.

The second impediment to this type of project is closely related to the first. The professor must also change. Because teaching people to think inevitably means teaching them to challenge, I had to make sure of my own psychological security and flexibility. Psychologically, I had to relinquish some of my omnipotence in the classroom. I also had to be flexible enough to forgo some of the content. I have not fully resolved the conflict between teaching content and analytical and creative thinking skills. But I am still working on a smooth integration of the two.

The teaching fellows program also represented for many of its participants the first opportunity to communicate concerns about teaching to colleagues. In my own case, I uncovered resources in the form of personnel and programs that I did not know existed at the university. The participants in the program have joined ranks to promote better teaching. I have presented my project to the political science faculty, and I am presenting a paper about the project at a national convention. I now find that I talk to my colleagues more about teaching. Both my students and I have improved.

References

Pye, L. *Politics, Personality, and Nation Building.* New Haven, Conn.: Yale University Press, 1962.

Curtina Moreland-Young is associate professor at Jackson State University, Mississippi. She is a former Rockefeller Fellow and Research Associate at the DuBois Institute at Harvard. Her main research interests are African politics and women in developing countries.

*High quality Computer-Assisted Instruction can be implemented
with a year's investigation and consultation.*

Computer-Assisted Instruction:
Getting Started and
Staying Compatible

Erich Lear

From the outset, the 1980–81 postdoctoral teaching fellows at Miami
University sought some common ground for genuine academic kin-
ship. We brought energetic initiative to individual goals but quickly
discovered our mutual concern about professional isolation. My experience parallels that of the group as a whole. Development of Computer-Assisted Instruction (CAI) drills in a music theory course, my project for the year, began as a personal professional interest that was sig-
nificantly enriched by the broader agenda of our compelling desire for
increased collegiality. However, speaking adequately of the need for
collegiality in this essay will be difficult, since addressing the issues of
developing Computer-Assisted Instruction is complex enough. CAI
perhaps will be more clearly understood if separated from the equally
complex description of the contributions of an academic community to
the success of such efforts. That these two aspects receive relatively distinct treatment here belies my true sentiment that collegiality is integral
to individual growth.

   One more introductory comment is in order. Pedagogical methods and tools are always controversial. Academics have already chosen

P. A. Lacey (Ed.). *Revitalizing Teaching Through Faculty Development.* New Directions
for Teaching and Learning, no. 15. San Francisco: Jossey-Bass, September 1983.

sides about the importance of CAI. Some feel that, five years from now, the entering university freshman class will be more computer literate on the whole than the faculty. Therefore, they have rushed ahead to become familiar with computer systems and methods of instruction themselves. Other academics may express their feelings about the importance of computer literacy more succinctly: So what?

To get started in CAI, you must simply want to. Any advocacy beyond that incites irrelevant debate. The extant literature is, to date, not sufficient to prove the superiority of computer applications over other pedagogical methods. However, there is such a general trend toward computer literacy that, unless you are at least familiar with the subject, you will not be able to enjoy watching others argue about it.

Getting Started

Information necessary to the beginner can be divided into two broad categories: (1) facts about equipment (hardware) and programs (software) that change rapidly as the technology expands and (2) problems of implementation that are similar regardless of application or the state of the art. The first category is intimidating; the second includes some considerations unique to CAI and some like those encountered in any pedagogical venture.

The best way to enter the flow of hardware and software information is to borrow (not buy) a computer and a few simple programs and actually do something—the "hands-on" approach. Borrowing can range from going to the nearest computer retailers and exploiting their salesmanship to arranging for a terminal owned by your institution to be placed in your office. Most retailers encourage prospective buyers to spend up to half an hour on a floor model, executing a demonstration program or two. Four or five such visits, coupled with a little reading, will give you enough information to comprehend any article in general readership publications—news magazines and general education journals. Such articles usually either report the extent of the educational stampede toward computer instruction and consequent pedagogical controversy, or they superficially survey the state of the art. Institutional facilities usually provide longer time blocks and a greater range of hardware and software than do retail outlets. In most cases, faculty, staff, or students familiar with the systems are available to help you. In addition, some institutions purchase tutorial programs for their computers that teach such subjects as beginning programming. These not only assist you in becoming familiar with their topics, they are also examples of CAI.

During this familiarization period you should encounter basic information about hardware and the standard terms: central processing units (cpu's or simply processors), various kinds of memory, input/output (I/O) devices (keyboards, screens, printers, and sound devices), and connecting equipment (cables and modems). Introductory descriptions of software should include: operating systems, general purpose packages (word processing, calculators, communications or interface programs, statistics, and data), programming languages (BASIC, Fortran, Pascal, and so on), and games. From my experience I would say that, for anyone employing the hands-on approach plus some reading, about three-to-five hours a week for a semester will provide general familiarization. Maintaining the currency of this material will require some effort; but, for the most part, important changes of a general nature will appear in the more specialized literature about applications appropriate to your interests.

Even during your initial investigations you will probably find some of the specialized equipment, programs, and publications applicable to your discipline. If you are the first at your institution to use computers in your area, then your research will, at first, rely more heavily on reading—both in computer journals and discipline-oriented journals—than on hands-on work. Specialized hardware and software will not be available. A check of recent discipline-oriented journals will often show an entire issue devoted to surveys and detailed discussions of computer use in your area.

To overcome the local lack of specialized materials, you could attend a workshop offered by professionals in your field (not vendors) dealing with computer use. In some cases, such workshops treat a broad range of computer applications when the market and state of the art justify such attention; in others, specific applications, and CAI in particular, are emphasized. Though weekend workshops cannot offer enough content to guide specialized investigations adequately, they are usually inspiring and offer some insight into how one group solved its problems. One-to-two week-long workshops usually provide in-depth coverage of where to find adequate equipment, an outline of computer use in the discipline, and a directory to the existing network of people, institutions, publications, and vendors involved in and supporting the use of computers in your field.

The national conventions of the National Educational Computer Consortium (NECC) and the Association for the Development of Computer Instructional Systems (ADCIS) include numerous vendor exhibits. General and specialized hardware and software are on display for several days. However, presentations are diverse in content. Attending such conventions will be most useful as an opportunity to see and briefly use the materials that you might previously have discussed at a workshop. This more specialized orientation will take another semester and perhaps a summer for the workshop. Maintaining familiarity with the newest developments in your field can be accomplished primarily through reading, though the national conventions of the NECC and ADCIS also serve this purpose.

CAI: Implementation

Armed with a year's modest investment of time and energy, you can now bring reasonably informed responses to the first and most important question in CAI implementation: What do I want to accomplish with the computer? The range of computer applications in education is already large. Those that fall into the CAI classification usually involve an interactive format — one in which the computer responds to input from the user, and vice versa, in such activities as drill and practice, simulation, and games.

While choosing one or another format for your application may seem to answer the "What do I want to do" question, that choice is only a partial answer. You may want the computer to actually teach some material, or you may only want to supplement your teaching with material on the computer. The main issue is the extent to which computer use will change the way you teach a given class. One extreme is to use computer drills as an optional study method, similar to worksheets or textbook assignments for which no grades are given. The other extreme is to require proficiency on specific material offered only on the computer that is necessary for completion of the course, with proficiency records maintained for each student by the computer. It is conceivable that an entire course could be delivered in this latter manner.

I believe that the most productive use of CAI should reflect both the limitations and the capabilities of your system. Computers cannot teach, but students can learn from them. High quality CAI will give a variety of feedback to the user, much of it similar to and based on the kinds of diagnostic and prescriptive efforts that teachers employ in classrooms. Your ability to evaluate the capabilities of CAI to do what you want it to do in your field will depend more on your ability as a teacher than on your familiarity with hardware and software.

Though evaluation of CAI is discipline-specific, some general observations are possible. The extent to which a given CAI package employs randomization in its presentation is often a good measure of quality. If a student can run the same lesson or problem ten times and not repeat any questions, or if the end goal of a simulation can be achieved through highly variable circumstances, then you are looking at more sophisticated CAI than if the same questions appear each time, attached to the same answers. As a general rule, the more refined a diagnosis the CAI can draw from the user's responses, the more sophisticated the program. Further, the more varied the prescriptions resulting from these diagnoses, the higher the quality of the CAI.

Some CAI packages offer the possibility of allowing the instructor to author some parts of the content. The most flexible of the programs that do this are called "authoring languages." Using an authoring language does not require the ability to program. Authoring languages are essentially "formatters": programs that allow you to choose any of several common methods for presenting material, store that material in the computer, and retrieve it later for presentation in the chosen format. Good authoring languages allow for the same kinds of diagnostic and prescriptive actions that good CAI packages do. One of the chief advantages of an authoring language is that, while only one person in a department may have extensive knowledge about computers, other faculty who are novices in computer use can write CAI material of good quality, simply by using their training and perception as teachers.

Another aspect of CAI implementation to be considered is the people and resources involved in operating and maintaining a system. As with libraries and laboratories, CAI facilities are used by students and faculty, are often monitored by staff, are housed in specially reserved areas with appropriate security, and require maintenance. The availability of the system to users on a regular schedule, the monitoring of system use by people capable of troubleshooting the system, and the provision of security for the data and programs in the system become increasingly important as the system becomes larger and more complex. The cost of telephone lines, area security, and repairs to the system will also increase as the system grows. Foresight in the disposition of such responsibilities and costs is essential to the success of your CAI application.

A final consideration is that of "system compatibility." For any of several reasons, you will eventually want your computer to communicate with another computer, or you will want to use a program originally written for another system. You may need compatibility with other campus systems for some work and compatibility with external systems for other work. Usually "interfacing" of this kind is either fairly easy to accomplish, through a communication device or program, or virtually impossible without rewriting the entire original program. In some cases, compatibility may be necessary only for certain parts of your system — for example, data storage — while specialized aspects can remain within your application. In any event, the technological developments expected in the next few years dictate a need to prepare for communications between systems. Fortunately, vendors are aware of this market necessity and seem to be offering increasingly flexible hardware and software to meet compatibility demands.

CAI: Consultation in an Academic Setting

The following discussion strongly advocates personal professional compatibility — the ability to make a case to a broad constituency in a controversial area such as the process of CAI implementation. The growing use of computers in academia has produced so many expensive and time-consuming methods that duplicate each other that administrators and faculty are justifiably suspicious of any proposal involving computers which does not demonstrate extensive consultation, both on and off campus. Such consultation can present so many roadblocks to implementation that an individual's interest and initiative are lost. Of course, committees, purchasing officers, fellow faculty, administrators, and students will, given the present academic climate, have a greater interest in proposals involving computers than in more traditional projects. Some will urge swift action to keep up with the educational state of the art; others will voice suspicions that computers will replace faculty in time and should therefore be assimilated slowly. Both positions reflect genuine concerns, but neither is sufficient for deciding an action. I believe that grounds for compatibility between these various interests can be found in three basic arguments for CAI implementation: (1) Computers and their applications provide a set of tools and the skills to use them, rather than an all-encompassing ideology; (2) some activities and information can be delivered faster on computers than in any other way; and (3) the cost is appropriate for the efficiency gained.

Although the first argument seems reasonable, many argue that the medium can change the message. Computer delivery could inadvertently change the students' perception of material. To meet such criticism positively will require solid pedagogical bases in the proposed system. Further, the reservations expressed about computer delivery focus on the same issues encountered in debates about which text among several to use for a particular course. A text can distort or falsify material; our job is to choose texts which do not. The same integrity is required of a good CAI proposal.

The second and third arguments go hand-in-hand. The speed of the computer in handling information is patently obvious. However, reaching a consensus among all parties concerned about the appropriateness of the costs involved is a different matter. For your own satisfaction, as well as for that of others participating in the decision-making process, you should make the attempt to compare the cost over time of your proposed computer application to the cost of a more traditional approach to the same goal. Such comparisons as the cost of computerization versus the cost of text books, photocopied hand-outs, duplicated worksheets, and inventory forms are useful and not too difficult to prepare. The comparison of the cost of personnel involved in a traditional method versus replacement of personnel time with computer use, on the other hand, is a far more sensitive issue. Any such proposal will meet careful scrutiny, especially in the current economic climate.

Though decision-making in academia can be torturously slow, a proposal enriched by broad consultation gains in stature and likelihood of success. An eagerness to include such input will generally be viewed in your favor. Given the controversial nature of Computer-Assisted Instruction, the benefits of proceeding in a thoroughly collegial manner cannot be overstated.

CAI: A Brief Personal History

The chronological progress of my own CAI project, although focused on development of music theory drills, may provide some assistance to those in other fields. I would reiterate that the real first step for me came from my personal interest in computerized methods of instruction, and that this interest was the force that produced continued action. Action motivated by educational expedience — or by the desire to be up-to-date — will not, I believe, yield the same high quality results.

In the fall of 1979, I applied unsuccessfully for a Miami University Instructional Improvement Fellowship to investigate computer use in music theory courses. At that time, I had only begun the general familiarization process outlined previously; as a result, my fellowship application was vague at best. The following spring a colleague on the music theory faculty, who was aware of my interest, referred me to a systems analysis major who had enrolled in this colleague's course for non-music majors. The student had inquired if any consideration ever had been given to using computers as a drill medium in theory courses. I asked the student to write brief programs in BASIC, using question formats and pedagogical methods suggested by me. The programs were stored and operated on the university's Hewlett Packard 3000 minicompurer, which is located in a central building on campus normally open twenty-four hours a day to students and faculty.

During this same period, my continued familiarization efforts had moved from general materials to music-oriented materials. Information clearly indicated extensive institutional and commercial activity at levels far beyond our local efforts. As a culmination of this familiarization process, I attended a two-week music theory CAI workshop at North Texas State University (Denton, Texas) in June of 1980. The target audience for this workshop was made up of people in the same circumstances as myself: near-novices hoping to introduce useful, good quality computer drills into their theory classes.

My 1980–81 teaching fellowship year included development of CAI as a teaching project. Given the commercial availability of highly-developed music CAI materials, this could have meant simply gaining approval to purchase a microcomputer and the appropriate software. But my vision for the project was based on what *I* wanted to do with computers — the first implementation questions. The goals of the Miami system were quite limited: to provide drill materials on music theory fundamentals, with primary emphasis on spelling exercises in short-answer format. The following goals that I had were therefore not part of the system agenda: presentation of new material, drill in aural recognition (ear training), data storage, or any research in connection with student or system behavior.

Virtually all commercially available systems provide one or more of those aspects listed as not among our system's goals. Since local development required relatively little expense, local development was clearly preferable in my case. The systems analysis student continued to assist with programming through April 1981, spending an average of three-to-five hours a week on the system during fall and spring semesters. My own knowledge of BASIC had advanced sufficiently by February 1981 so that I spent an equivalent three-to-five hours a week on programming, as well as format and pedagogy guidance. The number and refinement of the lessons now in the system also allowed for regular previewing by selected students. They provided suggestions for revisions in question content and format. Finally, the music theory committee discussed system progress and made plans for implementation.

During the year I applied once again for an Instructional Improvement Fellowship for summer 1981, and this time my application was successful. The fellowship period of May and June was sufficient time for final program revisions and testing. The drills were introduced into the fall 1981 freshman music theory class and continue to date as supplementary drill material for that course.

Collegiality

The primary objective here has been exposition of particular and general aspects of the initial steps in the implementation of Computer-Assisted Instruction. However, I would like to close with an observation about achieving collegiality. Like computer use, collegiality is a skill requiring development and practice. The Miami teaching fellows program incorporated a mentor system that, for me, provided some help in this development. A single senior faculty member, serving as an adviser, can foresee the kinds of hurdles that a junior perion needs to learn to negotiate. For the junior partner, individual cooperation of this kind provides an initial example of the advantages of close professional relationships.

Additional Sources

Arenson, M. "An Examination of Computer-Based Educational Hardware at Twenty-eight National Consortiums for Computer-Based Music Instruction Member Schools." *Journal of Computer-Based Instruction,* 1978, *5* (1 and 2), 38–44.

Arenson, M. "A Model for Systematic Revision of Computer-Based Instruction Materials." *Journal of Computer-Based Instruction,* 1981, *7* (3), 78–83.

Burson, J. "A Ten-Point-Seven Criteria CAI Materials Appraisal Process." *Proceedings of the National Conference of the Association for the Development of Computer Instructional Systems,* 1981, 131–136.

Mitzel, H. E. "On the Importance of Theory in Applying Technology to Education." *Journal of Computer-Based Instruction,* 1981, *7* (4), 93–98.

Music Educators Journal, 1983, *69* (5), entire issue.

Peters, G. D., and Eddins, J. M. *A Planning Guide to Successful Computer Instruction.* Champaign, Ill.: Electronic Courseware Systems, 1981.

Taylor, J. A., and Parrish, J. W. "A National Survey on the Uses of, and Attitudes Toward, Programmed Instruction and Computers in Public School and College Music Education." *Journal of Computer-Based Instruction,* 1978, *5* (1 and 2), 11–21.

*Erich Lear is assistant professor of music
at Miami University, Oxford, Ohio.*

For those of us who acknowledge that developmental processes occur in students during the college years, the question of what teaching methods foster development is an important one.

Teaching Philosophies and Methods: A Developmental Perspective

Carl E. Paternite

As recently as four or five years ago I would have thought the title for the present chapter an unlikely one for a volume on new directions for teaching and learning. In fact, I probably would have dismissed the suggestion that I could contribute anything to such a volume. My surprise back then certainly would not have been due to a lack of interest in college teaching. Rather, it would have arisen because of the perspective on the teaching enterprise I had at the time—a perspective that has shifted dramatically over the past four academic years, largely due to my experiences as a postdoctoral teaching fellow during the 1980–81 academic year. As a teaching fellow, I was able to examine, along with colleagues from diverse disciplines, both my teaching philosophy and my methods for the classroom. My fellowship year was extremely valuable, because it stimulated thought about innovative teaching that is reflected in my current thinking.

Teaching Philosophies Within a Developmental Context

When people ask me what kind of psychologist I am, I usually refer to myself as a "developmental-clinician." In part, this designation reflects my graduate education, which had a combined focus on devel-

P. A. Lacey (Ed.). *Revitalizing Teaching Through Faculty Development*. New Directions for Teaching and Learning, no. 15. San Francisco: Jossey-Bass, September 1983.

opmental and clinical psychology. More importantly, the designation reflects my commitment to a developmental view of people in general — and of people who are experiencing difficulties in particular. Basically, I acknowledge that individuals are active architects of their worlds, and that the ways in which people construe or make meaning of their worlds can change in a predictable sequence over the course of their lives. An important corollary of these views is that experience with the environment (for example, how we interact with our family or with our peers) can create dissonances in our view of the world that stimulate development. This general perspective on the concept of development is reflected in the elaborately detailed theories of developmentalists such as Kegan (1982), Loevinger (1976), and Perry (1970).

My developmental views have had a strong impact for some time on my activities as a psychotherapist, on my research involvement, and on the content of what I teach in my undergraduate and graduate courses. However, in spite of my professional background, my developmental perspective has not had a conscious impact on the process of my teaching (that is, how I teach what I teach) until recently. I believe I entered the enterprise of college teaching as if I was oblivious, at least on a conscious level, to the fact that college students — like children, adolescents, and older adults — are actively engaged in processes of personal development that have important implications for the college classroom. In her review of models of college education, Goldenberger (1982) offers a characterization of faculty that fits my assumptions as a new professor in the late 1970s. She suggests that "the prevailing attitude among college faculty, particularly those teaching large classes, is that their job is to profess; it is up to the student to listen and learn" (p. 235). Goldenberger goes on to suggest that faculty, for the most part, are neither very interested in nor well-informed about the ways in which students change and develop over the college years. As a result, faculty are often oblivious to the discrepancy between what they think they profess (teach) and what the developmental beings on the other side of the lectern take away with them from the classroom. Other theorists, most notably Perry (1970, 1981), have written at length about this gulf between what we think we teach and what our developing students are able to receive from our teaching. In the opening pages of his 1970 book on the intellectual and ethical development of college students, Perry provides a compelling example, which suggests that three students in a given class may construe a lecture in three dramatically different ways according to the interrelated intellectual and ethical developmental levels attained by the students.

Once the developmental needs of our students are acknowledged as appropriate subjects for us to consider, a host of teaching issues become relevant to us. We begin to experience a permanent discomfort with print-outs of means and standard deviations from end-of-course student evaluations as sources of knowledge about our students, their needs, and their capacities. Perry (1981) suggests that means and standard deviations may in fact conceal important treasures. If we approach teaching from a developmental perspective, what becomes relevant is the richness of variability in student feedback and the great diversity among students that can be found in virtually every college course.

In spite of reasonably strong mean evaluations for a given course, students in that course can evaluate the same experience very differently, with one calling it "the most meaningful and important experience of my college career" and another describing it as "a real rip-off, an absolute waste of time and effort." In the past I certainly felt that, even as good instructors, we are unable to please everyone and it is enough that most of our students will be reasonably satisfied with our instruction. Nevertheless, I now believe that it is a mistake to view student satisfaction or dissatisfaction primarily as a reflection of static characteristics such as motivation or willingness to work. More constructive attempts to explain the impact we have in the classroom must consider students' developmental stages in relation to the process issues of instruction.

In the remainder of the present chapter I will focus on my efforts to examine how instruction works in developmental context. Given my developmental interests, I have offered undergraduate psychology courses like "Adolescent Development" and "Developmental Psychology of the College Student" several times over the past four years. The latter course is a new departmental offering that I developed. The content of the courses, by definition, has a very personal meaning for all students enrolled, since all have struggled with or are still struggling with adolescent developmental issues. Students are studying what they are, what they are becoming, and what frees or blocks them in their lives. How they are asked to approach that material can, in turn, free or block them. These two courses have provided an ideal setting for examining the teaching process from a developmental perspective. Not every course we teach has so obvious a connection between content and process, but I am confident that the general perspective and the teaching and learning issues and solutions that I describe below have relevance for a wide range of courses and classrooms.

Teaching-Learning Issues

The heterogeneity in our classes can be refreshing but also serves as a source of frustration when we try to think through the possibility of having a positive impact on most or all of our students. The most difficult question then is: In light of the developmental heterogeneity of the students enrolled in our courses, how can we hope to have a positive impact on most of them? To arrive at useful answers to this question involves considering several issues, including the definition of the term *impact*, the philosophical position one takes toward appropriate goals and objectives for courses, and the practical matters of course design and teaching methods.

Everything I have to say here is based on my commitment to a liberal arts perspective in the college classroom. Widick and Simpson (1978) suggest that this perspective implies that students not only should learn facts but also should be encouraged to "formulate a humane value system, integrate a world view, and develop a broader understanding of self and others" (p. 28). Translated into course objectives and goals, such a perspective dictates a commitment on the part of the instructor to both students' course-specific content mastery and to their personal development in general.

Course Design and Methods

In the courses I have worked on, both the content and teaching process have been developmental. My choices of content — with a three-way focus on theory, research, and practical issues — have emphasized a wide variety of personality and cognitive developmental models. The writings of a number of theorists provide the framework for course units on such topics as autonomy, competence, identity, intimacy, cognitive development, and contemporary adjustment issues (for example, drug use and suicide). My choices of procedures or methods for teaching this content have been influenced strongly by the cognitive developmental theory proposed by Perry (1970), and the instructional applications of the theory proposed by such researchers as Knefelkamp (1974), Stephenson and Hunt (1977), and Widick and Simpson (1978).

The theory or scheme of cognitive development proposed by Perry (1970) is relevant to the college classroom because it suggests a strong link between developmental level — or readiness — of the college student and the learning process. In the Perry scheme, cognitive development of the college student is charted along nine qualitatively distinct, sequential positions. These positions reflect different assumptions by students about the nature of knowledge and values, and, as a result, their different understandings about what they are doing when they are learning what the course offers. In the opening chapter of his 1970 book, Perry characterizes these nine positions as reflecting "the structures that the students explicitly or implicitly impute to the world, especially those structures in which they construe the nature and origins of knowledge, of values, and of responsibility" (p. 1). Simply stated, the paradigm of developmental movement for a student is from a simplistic, categorical, unqualified, polar (right-wrong, good-bad) view of knowledge and values to a view of knowledge and values that is complex, pluralistic, and contingent — and then eventually to a view of knowledge and values that reflects personal commitment within a relativistic context. Perry and others have referred to these three developmental tiers as *dualism, contextual relativism*, and *commitment in relativism*, respectively. For the interested reader, vivid portrayals of this developmental progression are provided in a number of Perry's works (1970, 1978, 1981).

In their discussion of the implications of the Perry developmental scheme for the college classroom, Widick and Simpson (1978) suggest that, in its purest form, *dualism* is reflected by a student who not only views all classifiable knowledge as either absolutely right or wrong but also views her task as a learner to be that of finding and knowing the "right" answers. For such a student, encounters with diversity, interpretive and comparative tasks, and self-directed, independent learning are stressful, and the students are usually very grade-conscious. On the other hand, *relativism* is reflected by a student who views knowledge as contextual. She sees her task as a learner to be that of understanding the "rightness" of answers within their context. For this student, encounters with diversity, interpretive and comparative tasks, and self-directed, independent learning are viewed as desirable aspects of a course. Thus, according to the application model of Widick and Simpson (1978) the content-specific mastery and personal development of these two types of students in a given course will be encouraged by different teaching methods, which serve as supports and challenges to the students.

The two-fold goals of content-mastery and personal development are encouraged in the dualistic student by such teaching supports as emphasis on instructor-directed and instructor-structured learning activities — what is called high course structure — and emphasis on a warm atmosphere in the classroom. Course challenges such as inclusion of diverse, conflicting content, instructional procedures emphasizing analytic skills, and emphasis on direct experiential learning, also benefit this student. However, content mastery and personal development are encouraged in the relativistic student by an emphasis on student-directed learning activities — low course structure. In addition, for such a student attainment of course goals is encouraged by challenges such as extensive emphasis on diverse, conflicting content and analytic skills and emphasis on indirect, abstract learning.

My overgeneralized discussion of college student intellectual development and classroom applications may lead the reader to view development in a static and much too linear way. Clearly, when we reflect on our own lives and those of students we have known well, it is evident that development is neither static nor linear. Perry (1981) applies the metaphor of a helix to characterize the recursive nature of development. However, with cautions against static and linear inferences in mind, it is still possible to think of instructional methods from a developmental perspective that might differentially affect our developmentally heterogenous students.

Teaching-Learning Solutions

Through various combinations of adjustments to our instruction, in the form of different supports and challenges, it is possible to increase the chances of reaching the major developmental groupings of students within a given course. In my "Adolescent Development" and "Developmental Psychology of the College Student" courses I have experimented with a variety of instructional methods. Consistent with the conceptualization of instructional variables proposed by Widick and Simpson (1978), I will focus here on two categories of support strategies and two categories of challenge strategies.

Personalism in the Classroom as a Support. I have never been disappointed by the educational effects of supporting an informal, personal atmosphere in my courses. Widick and Simpson (1978) offer the following rationale for such an emphasis, suggesting that "for all students, development and learning can be risky ventures. Our knowledge of how people cope suggests that students need an instructional atmosphere that encourages such risk-taking. Thus, an environment characterized by a high degree of trust between students and teacher and an attitude of cooperative learning would seem to be very important" (p. 37). Perry (1981) expresses a similar rationale in a slightly different manner by referring to the educator's responsibility as a person to hear and honor the pains of growth in her students. Perry argues that "the instructor can serve as a bridge linking the old self with the new: 'He knew me when, and he knows me now'" (p. 109).

A commitment to personalism in a course does not imply staged showmanship, as is occasionally seen in those who are overly conscious of wanting to entertain their classes. In fact, I believe that such showmanship actually impersonalizes the classroom by creating a wall between the students and the performer-entertainer-instructor, who figuratively hides behind the lectern. A constructive commitment to a warm, personal atmosphere implies viewing learning as a cooperative interchange in which the instructor is available to students in the classroom in a spontaneous, uncontrived way.

It is difficult and potentially misleading to list just one or two specific examples of personalism, since there are many ways that it can be evidenced in and out of the classroom. In my particular courses it has been meaningful to me to share personal experiences and anecdotes from my own life, since they relate to our focus on particular adolescent and college student development topics. In addition, outside of the classroom, the way I use office hours has provided me with rich opportunities to build an atmosphere of personalism. Office hours can be more than a forum for the instructor to clarify a student's confusion about a point made in yesterday's lecture or to argue with a student about why she earned only partial credit for one of her answers on the last examination. Office hours, which I strongly and persistently urge students to make use of, provide an excellent opportunity for the instructor to develop a better understanding of a number of things relevant to particular students — such as how the course relates to other educational experiences of the students, why the course is being taken, and what aspects of the course have had a particular impact on students. Generally speaking, such information can help the instructor to better understand the gulf between what she thinks is being taught in the course and what students actually hear and understand. More importantly, it can help students appreciate that the instructor is interested in and committed to making the course affect their personal development and learning directly.

Course Structure as a Support. Having now offered "Adolescent Development" five times and "Developmental Psychology of the College Student" twice since 1979, I have experimented with varying degrees of instructor-imposed structure for the courses. Striving for a balance between high and low structure is important in that the instructor wants to provide support not only for the student who thrives on externally-guided learning but also for the student whose content mastery and development are encouraged by self-directed learning. The balance between high and low structure that has evolved in my courses might best be described as "structure with options." My courses are highly-structured by detailed syllabi that include elaborate descriptions of the goals and objectives, requirements, and instructional procedures. In addition, the syllabi include day-by-day schedules for the topics to be covered, the assigned readings, due dates for additional outside assignments, and examination dates. However, students discover considerable flexibility in the course structure, which they are invited to use. For example, I inform students that not only are the overall course content schedules subject to revision as we proceed, but also that the latter half of the course schedules (including what topics we will cover and when we will cover them) are subject to revision based on their suggestions. When we approach the midpoint of the semester I actively solicit suggestions for changes and then develop a revised content outline for the remainder of the semester.

A second example of structure with options involves term paper assignments. In each of my courses I routinely assign several brief term papers, with the specific due dates and grading criteria described for each. Additional structure for these brief papers is provided by asking students to focus, in some way, on a broadly defined topic. However, students are encouraged to define the topics more narrowly based on their own interests and expertise, and they are invited to use me as a resource to develop the topics. A third example involves inviting students, on a limited individual basis, to propose and negotiate optional assignments, in lieu of those assignments proposed on the syllabi. For example, an additional major term paper might substitute for an in-class examination, or a nontraditional project such as a video production might substitute for a written term paper. In my experience, only a very small percentage of students propose such options, but for those who do, assuming that their motivations are understood and that they receive guidance from the instructor, the choice can increase the match between the instructor's goals and the student's content mastery and developmental needs.

Course Content as a Challenge. In order to encourage the content mastery and personal development of not only dualistic-thinking students but also those who appreciate the contextual relativism of knowledge, diversity in the forms course content takes is important. In my case, diversity of form and content are provided by readings, lectures, audiovisual presentations, and classroom discussions of content of a theoretical, empirical, and practical nature. For instance, in covering the topic of identity, I ask students to read works by identity theorists, research on the topic of identity development, and biographical materials such as case studies and biographies. In concert with this reading, in-class activities emphasize theoretical, empirical, and practical material, including some sharing of personal experiences by students. In addition, diversity in content involves the selection of specific content within each of these broad areas. For example, I routinely select some uncritical, descriptive content and some that is more analytical and comparative. Thus, for the student who feels a need for the crutch of certainty some accommodation is provided, and yet the limits of that certainty are introduced. In addition, for the student more directly immersed in contextualism, the analytical content encourages further development of critical thinking.

Learning Activities as a Challenge. Challenges also can be provided by the learning activities that are emphasized in a course. In my courses I have striven for a balance between an emphasis on experiential and abstract learning activities. In addition to lectures that include both descriptive and analytical content, other important learning activities such as structured instructor-led discussion, less structured student-led group discussions, and student self-study journals are part of the courses.

Instructor-led discussion provides an excellent opportunity to influence the balance between an experiential and an indirect, analytical focus. For example, the instructor might choose to pose a self-study question to the class: "What was it like for you as a fifteen-year-old?" Or, as either a follow-up or in lieu of this question, the instructor might pose a combined experiential-analytical question: "What would theorist X have to say about your experiences as a fifteen-year-old?" An even more analytical question might be: "Imagine a debate between theorists X and Y that concerns your experiences as a fifteen-year-old. In what ways would they agree and disagree?"

Less structured, student-led discussions, on the other hand, can provide educational challenge by allowing students to encourage each other to be self-disclosing, self-critical, and analytical at the same time. On class days when brief term papers are due, I routinely ask students to break into small groups of four or five people in order to read and discuss their papers. Students are told that this is an opportunity for them to learn not only what some of their peers are thinking about but also how their own ideas are viewed by these same peers. Given the latitude to define the focus of the group discussion more specifically on their own, these small groups, through the challenges and supports they provide to members, are quite valuable.

An additional learning activity, which I am extremely interested in further developing in the future, is the use of self-study journals. Student journals are especially appropriate in the type of developmental psychology courses I have been describing throughout this chapter. They are also potentially useful in a wide variety of other courses. The intent of the journal is to help students, on a continuous basis throughout the semester, think about the applications of the material studied to their own lives. For each topic covered in my courses (for example, emancipation from parents and career choices), I prepare a self-study exercise that students complete on their own and compile in a journal. Students are also encouraged to make additional journal entries when their thoughts are stimulated by the course content. Twice during the semester, journals are turned in so that I can offer written comments on their entries. The journals are graded, as I describe clearly at the outset, on a pass-fail basis — with a "pass" awarded for mere completion of the journal. Specific content of entries in the journal is not graded. This loosely structured journal assignment, which students are free to take as seriously as they like, provides an opportunity to personalize the course and emphasizes its relevance to the student. In addition, through the instructor's written comments about specific journal entries, it is possible to stress the balance between experiential and abstract learning, depending on an assessment of what might best challenge a particular student.

Concluding Comments

At the end of a recent semester, and after grades were determined, one of my students from a section of the "Developmental Psychology of the College Student" course handed me a note that included the following:

> Thank you very much for allowing me to understand myself better and to learn about college student development and the responsibility that a commitment holds and how I've responded to a commitment. This is one course that does affect my life from here on out. It couldn't have come at a better time. Maybe it was fate. I picked this course at late registration because of the time period. What a stroke of genius it was!

This student's comments lead to my two closing points. First, I firmly believe that our courses can have strong effects, in terms of both content mastery and personal development, on most of our students. Second, and more importantly, my experience suggests that the extent of the effect courses have on students does not have to remain a matter of fate.

References

Goldenberger, N. R. "Developmental Assumptions Underlying Models of General Education." *Liberal Education,* 1982, *67* (1), 233–243.

Kegan, R. *The Evolving Self: Problem and Process in Human Development.* Cambridge, Mass.: Harvard University, 1982.

Knefelkamp, L. "Developmental Instruction: Fostering Intellectual and Personal Growth." Unpublished doctoral dissertation, Department of Psychology, University of Minnesota, 1974.

Loevinger, J. *Ego Development.* San Francisco: Jossey-Bass, 1976.

Perry, W. G., Jr. *Forms of Intellectual and Ethical Development in the College Years: A Scheme.* New York: Holt, Rinehart and Winston, 1970.

Perry, W. G., Jr. "Sharing in the Costs of Growth." In C. A. Parker (Ed.), *Encouraging Development in College Students.* Minneapolis: University of Minnesota, 1978.

Perry, W. G., Jr. "Cognitive and Ethical Growth: The Making of Meaning." In A. W. Chickering and Associates (Eds.), *The Modern American College.* San Francisco: Jossey-Bass, 1981.

Stephenson, B. W., and Hunt, C. "Intellectual and Ethical Development: A Dualistic Curriculum Intervention for College Students." *The Counseling Psychologist,* 1977, *6* (4), 39–42.

Widick, C., and Simpson, D. "Development Concepts in College Instruction." In C. A. Parker (Ed.), *Encouraging Development in College Students.* Minneapolis: University of Minnesota, 1978.

Carl E. Paternite is a clinical psychology faculty member and director of the Psychology Clinic in the Department of Psychology of Miami University. During the 1980–81 academic year he was a Lilly Endowment postdoctoral teaching fellow.

A teaching fellows program on campus provides a powerful resource for increasing an institution's excellence.

Ripples on the Pond: A Teaching Fellows Program Examined

Walter L. Barker

Administrators searching for ways to improve the quality of their institutions should consider what a teaching fellows program can do to help them achieve that goal. It can offer older teachers an opportunity to rethink and change their teaching. It can provide new instructors with the skills and strategies they need to be effective teachers from the beginning of their careers. It can help students learn the thinking skills and modes of analysis they need to survive in a world of expanding knowledge. It can contribute to the intellectual life of a campus by opening up new areas for faculty research as well as by providing a forum for teachers from different disciplines to participate in a common dialogue. Because it helps to impose intellectual structure on teaching, it can provide administrators with better means to evaluate and control the effectiveness of campus teaching. And, since teachers who learn these new skills inevitably share them with other teachers, the dividends of a teaching fellows program are far greater than the original costs.

P. A. Lacey (Ed.). *Revitalizing Teaching Through Faculty Development.* New Directions for Teaching and Learning, no. 15. San Francisco: Jossey-Bass, September 1983.

Looking Back

Of course, administrators have not had this choice for long. The oldest programs designed for any systematic training of teaching assistants and junior faculty were begun only fifteen to twenty years ago. They are still so few and unusual that they stand out like fresh saplings on a barren landscape. The Lilly Endowment's postdoctoral teaching fellows program was one of the first programs to confront this neglect and it is only ten years old. Consequently, the majority of faculty now teaching in American colleges and universities have never been prepared for classroom instruction beyond a primitive level.

I came of teaching age in that older system when college administrators acted as though they believed participation in a graduate program automatically conferred pedagogical competence on researchers. The perception by faculty that academia's most tangible rewards and highest intellectual status were given for doing research helped to discourage a formal study of college teaching. I never knew any older teachers who were prompted to read about college instruction as an intellectual subject separate from their academic specialties. Furthermore, as conversations in faculty centers would seem to attest, very few college instructors ever mention classroom life at all except to report on some student irregularities. For generations campus knowledge about another teacher's course came from second-hand sources. Administrators and senior teachers considered it bad form to look in on new teachers or even to ask inexperienced instructors to discuss their teaching.

In any case, most faculty could not even talk intelligently about pedagogy. Most college teachers do not have a well-thought-out notion of what they actually do in a classroom. Most believe that the key to excellent teaching lies somewhere in the elusive nature of personality. Or they assume that good teaching is only a measure of popularity with students; those who can do it have been blessed by the gods and those who cannot should be thinking — after they get tenure — of transferring over to some better-paying administrative position. In those days, administrators, teachers, and students alike seemed to leave good teaching to chance — but at a terrible cost. Even though Gilbert Highet, in *The Immortal Profession* (1976), praises great teachers by calling attention to the awe and affection they have evoked from fortunate students, his focus obscures the incompetent and damaging teaching that students have suffered for generations. When I began my college teaching, in 1961, course staffing was considered such a low priority that some administrators reacted to unexpected needs by practically bring-

ing in people off the street. For example, one day I happened to run into the department chairman while walking across the campus. Because
he knew I was taking some graduate courses, he asked me if I might be
interested in teaching two sections of "Introduction to Literature,"
scheduled to begin in two days. Feeling flattered, I said, "Yes." And so
I was initiated unceremoniously into the mysteries of college teaching.

Although I liked literature, I could then imagine no way of
teaching a class, beyond trying to sound as brilliant and nonchalant as
my favorite teachers. Some published help was available for new instructors even then, such as Highet's *The Art of Teaching* (1950) and
McKeachie's *Teaching Tips* ([1951], 1978), now in its seventh edition.
But I did not know of them, nor did any of my teachers or other teaching assistants. I entered my first classroom armed only with the chairman's avuncular "Don't worry. You will do well."

I am not at all sure I did do well. Those first courses I taught
had a few golden moments, but usually only when my conversational
skills saw me through some good discussions. I had no clearly defined
sense of purpose and no notion of how to teach, other than to tell my
students what I thought were the most important facts and ideas about
each successive work. In retrospect, it seems clear that the teaching I
was doing in those days generated the kind of knowledge I needed for
my own studies more than it served the needs of my students. And so I
went from year to year, gradually learning how to embellish my presentation with theatrical liveliness. Even though I was concerned that
most students were passive learners, I spent most of my time lecturing.
When I did use some Socratic questioning, it was to lead students to
my understanding of a work, which I in turn had gleaned mostly from
critics and teachers. In my examinations I stressed learning through
memorization and, because I had no other way of evaluating students,
measured their performances against my own knowledge.

Yet I seemed to be a successful teacher. Students apparently
liked my classes and showed up in flattering numbers. My colleagues
passed on occasional praise from second-hand sources, and in the
annual reviews my chairman was kind enough to mention my teaching
as exceptionally fine. So when the University of Rhode Island's
Instruction Development Program announced its 1979–80 teaching fellows program and invited me to accept a fellowship, I felt perplexed. I
knew at the time that the university had an instructional development
program, but I had assumed that it was designed for new teachers and
for some older faculty who needed help in remedying their poor teaching. Ordinarily I would have declined the invitation, because I thought

most discussion about teaching to be vacuous and self-serving. But, since I had just agreed to serve a term as supervisor of teaching assistantships for the English Department, I accepted the offer. After all, I did need to pick up a vocabulary for talking about teaching and I could always add a new wrinkle or two to my classroom repertory. I even imagined, as I wrote my letter of acceptance, that I might dazzle some of my junior fellows with an example of my own pedagogical footwork.

This silly hubris did not last long in the urbane and informed discussions of our meetings. When the coordinator asked us to describe our philosophies of teaching, I felt uncomfortable, since I had never formulated one before. When some of the other fellows asked me to state the goals and objectives of my most popular course, I was not sure I knew the difference between the terms. And when I did venture forth a few statements about my teaching, they sounded strangely empty and fragile — something about my wanting students to learn some concepts, to know something or other about literature, and to appreciate what they had read.

Obviously, I had never thought critically about the pedagogical language I had been using for years and about how much it lacked the precision I had attributed to it. Gradually I came to see that my understanding of teaching was rooted in the language of my discipline. I did not know there could be a way of thinking that distinguished the process of teaching and learning from the product of knowledge. The implicit understanding of teaching I acted upon was that knowledge is a quantitative entity that can be put out there in the classroom and that students somehow take it into their heads unchanged. I never thought that students might not understand long sections of my lectures or that they might be hearing patterns of emphasis in these lectures that were different from what I intended. If a difference did show up between what I said and what they heard, I assumed that the problem was theirs — and that they were inattentive, not prepared, or perhaps a bit over their heads in my course.

Even as I completed the teaching fellows program in May 1980, I was aware of how it had provided me with the most sustained period of intellectual intensity since writing my dissertation. The excitement came from my exposure to new ideas, the mastering of new skills, and the discussion of my discoveries with other interested faculty. Over the course of the program I radically reconceptualized my role in the classroom. Understanding more about what learning is like from the inside of the student experience has led me to visualize the classroom more as a student-centered place than a content-oriented one. Part of that understanding comes from what is for me a new teaching principle:

Students as well as teachers and administrators are apt to learn more if they know what the intended purpose and purported significance of material is, along with what they should be able to do with their learning when they finish a course of study.

I now tell my students how a course's objectives are designed to achieve its goals. I explain to them what they should be able to do with the knowledge and the skills they will learn in the course. I provide them with frequent and varied opportunities to practice analytical skills so that they can perfect them. I make sure they get frequent feedback from me so that we can both monitor their progress. I shape quizzes and examinations to measure student mastery of the class objectives. I give them some sample questions and, in some cases, provide them with actual exam questions. In general, I try to use these skills at the same time that I continue to teach literature. But, at any rate, my classes have more structure than they did in the past; students talk more and seem to value their own participation, and I spend much more time preparing for class than I have in the past.

Beyond the Teaching Fellows Program

This new knowledge about teaching did not stay bound up in my classes for long. Because of my role as supervisor of the teaching assistants in my department, I was able to communicate this knowledge to new instructors. If the educational quality of an institution can be improved by older faculty changing their teaching styles, it is also important that new instructors learn something about the principles of effective teaching at the onset of their careers. Assuming a beginning pedagogical age of twenty-five, new instructors have a teaching life of some eighty semesters ahead of them.

As with the older faculty, a teaching assistant needs the time and resources to learn and practice teaching skills. And he needs to do this while he is trying to pass his own courses, study for comprehensives, write a thesis or dissertation, pay rent, worry about loans and jobs, and struggle to maintain the appearance of sanity. Asking a new teacher to master some of the rudiments of teaching may seem impossibly ambitious, but the task is not necessarily burdensome when it comes slowly, as it did for the teaching fellows, and is absorbed bit by bit. I have also discovered from my talks with teaching assistants just how much they appreciate having a sense of direction and purpose in the classroom. Their structured preparation helps to relieve some of the pressure and anxiety they feel about teaching by turning vague assumptions into explicit standards that can be met.

Equally important to the development of new teachers is having access to an experienced faculty member, someone they can go to while practicing their new craft. They are usually comforted to find out that teaching problems can be described in language that separates the act of teaching from the discipline being taught and that alternative strategies can be prescribed for specific problems. For example, about a year ago a teaching assistant confided to me that he was disappointed with his present students because they seemed more passive and less interested than those who were in his classes the previous semester. After finding that he did almost all the talking in class, I described the group discussion method to him and explained how effective it had proved in getting students to talk in my courses, to become active learners, and to share with me the responsibility for the learning that took place in the classroom. Three weeks later, during which time he came back twice to get material on questioning strategies, he invited me to sit in on his class. His students were animated and leaned forward to argue their points. They showed little embarrassment as they groped for greater clarity and precision. They beamed with pleasure when they offered conclusions that impressed the instructor. The teaching assistant in turn was pleased with his ability to solve a teaching problem that three weeks earlier he could not even define. And I, only one year earlier, would not have recognized in his idle comment a specific problem either. I remember having made the same comment myself in the past and have heard it many times from colleagues over the years.

Some Unexpected "Ripple" Effects

My teaching fellowship also led to new kinds of teaching assignments and opened up to me a new area for research and publication. A colleague in the Language Department, hearing that I was studying college instruction, asked me to help him design a course that could teach the analytical thinking skills used in the humanities to a group of Honors Program freshmen. As a result of our numerous discussions, he became a teaching fellow the following year. The course itself, judging from student response and a formal evaluation by the director of Instructional Development, was both popular and effective. And because of this success we were asked to adapt the course to the special needs of the university's adult education program and to teach analytical thinking skills in both an introductory class and an upper-level seminar.

This course had even more ripple effects. In my regular literature classes now, I make students explicitly aware of the thinking patterns used in the explication of literature at the same time that I present them with traditional content. I have gradually developed a strategy for describing the thinking patterns of literary characters based on Perry's (1970) pioneering study of intellectual development. By focusing student attention on the thinking process, I have found that students see more clearly how their own thinking patterns, consciously and unconsciously, organize and interpret their experience of self and world. Encouraged by the director of the Instructional Development Program, I delivered papers on this method for three successive years at the New England Conference on Teaching Students to Think.

I began to venture even farther afield. I team taught a comparative course on Italian and English literature. I was invited to be a guest lecturer in the Women's Study Program and in classes on human sexuality. I audited classes in art history and in the Italian language. In short, I was taking risks I had never attempted before. The fellowship gave me the confidence to teach in front of other teachers and to describe at professional forums what I was actually doing in a classroom. Paradoxically, the changes I have gone through have made my teaching more controlled and creative — more ordered and exciting.

The University-Wide Impact of the Fellowship Program

As I have talked to other teaching fellows during the past two years, I have come to appreciate just how much the program is helping to raise the level of university excellence. By the end of this current year, seventy-one full-time faculty will have completed the fellowship program. That amounts to about 10 percent of the entire university faculty. These figures will grow each year as long as the program and its popularity continue, the cost having been assumed by the university after three years of grant sponsorship. In countless discussions in offices and corridors, these fellows are beginning to affect the way their colleagues perceive a department's teaching goals.

Some of them are administering programs that influence the quality of teaching in multisectional classes. One recent teaching fellow is coordinating the introductory math course and is sharing with the staff some of the teaching skills and strategies he developed through the program for mathematics. Another has become chairman of the Chemistry Department and has instituted a two-and-one-half–day workshop for new lab assistants. He also persuaded the department's laboratory supervisor to attend the university's regular five-day Instructional Development Workshop. The supervisor now incorporates teaching strategies into the weekly meetings he holds with all teaching assistants assigned to freshman lab sections. Not content to rest with this change, the chairman is presently working with the university's Instructional Development staff on a plan to incorporate intellectual development factors into a curriculum model for chemistry, the end result of which is to motivate student interest and to teach them the scientific method through problem solving. The chairman's ability to stir up interest in college teaching is such that this year's group of teaching fellows includes four faculty members from the Chemistry Department.

Teaching fellows here at the University of Rhode Island are also beginning to make major contributions to administrative policies and decisions that touch the entire campus. Some are raising educational issues in the faculty senate where their fellowships have won a new legitimacy for them. Some are serving on such groups as the Committee on General Education and the Committee for Effective Teaching. One former fellow, whose ideal educational institution would identify and match student learning styles with faculty teaching styles, has left his department to become an assistant dean of the University College. During his brief tenure there, he developed a workshop that helps students cope with teachers who do not provide them with course objectives and sample exam questions. He teaches them the skills they need to talk to teachers about classroom expectations, to ask specific questions designed to elicit course objectives from instructors, and, finally, to construct exam questions from this knowledge. Unfortunately, administrators are often forced to waste valuable resources and time contending with the underside of college teaching, an unwanted legacy from the *laissez-faire* past.

Conclusions

An administration that provides its faculty with a teaching fellows program enhances the professional and humanistic worth of its institution. The program can raise the effectiveness of an institution because it helps students, teachers, and administrators gain greater control over the educational process. It provides faculty and administrators with a reliable knowledge base for making informed assessments and decisions about teaching. It gives older faculty a chance to change, to become more versatile, and to make more valuable contributions to a school. This is crucial when so many administrators are tempted by constricting budgets to contract out individual courses to part-time teachers who travel from campus to campus, uncommitted to any one institution. When its permanent faculty does gain a reputation for good teaching, an institution becomes much more competitive in these days of diminishing student numbers. Similarly, on the departmental level, good teaching in the introductory courses can attract more students to major in a subject or to return for elective credits.

In addition to these pragmatic benefits, an instructional development program offers some immeasurable subjective and humanistic gifts to a college campus. It ensures, through its "ripple" effect, the inevitable formation and wide dissemination of higher standards of teaching and learning. It provides a powerful validation for college teaching by signaling to faculty that their teaching is important and that striving toward instructional improvement is a worthy goal. As almost every recipient will attest, a teaching fellows program, by virtue of its common discourse, breaks down the distancing walls of specialization. And in so doing, it helps a faculty experience an energizing sense of collegiality and to recover a lost definition of the word *university*. In a future not too far away, some of the most imaginative curricula of twenty-first century will be designed by former teaching fellows.

References

Highet, G. *The Art of Teaching.* New York: Knopf, 1950.

Highet, G. *The Immortal Profession: The Joys of Teaching and Learning.* New York: Weybright and Talley, 1976.

McKeachie, W. J. *Teaching Tips: A Guidebook for the Beginning College Teacher.* Lexington, Mass.: Heath, 1978. (Originally published 1951.)

Perry, W. G., Jr. *Forms of Intellectual and Ethical Development in the College Years.* New York: Holt, Rinehart and Winston, 1970.

Walter L. Barker is an associate professor in the English Department at the University of Rhode Island, where he teaches the standard undergraduate and graduate courses in literature. He is a past coordinator of the school's Honors Program and has also taught in its Talent Development and Adult Programs.

This profile of a Lilly postdoctoral teaching awards program focuses on what was learned through administering the grant and the impact the program had on individual faculty, departments, and the institution.

A Profile of a Postdoctoral Teaching Program

Thomas M. Schwen
Mary Deane Sorcinelli

In 1974 the Lilly Endowment, Inc., proposed a postdoctoral teaching awards program and invited colleges and universities to submit proposals for programs that would introduce junior, untenured faculty to the profession of teaching. In early 1979 Indiana University, Bloomington, designed and proposed a faculty development program and was selected to participate for a three-year grant period, which was extended for an unprecedented fourth year. As director and associate director of the Lilly fellowship program, we have guided the program from its inception to its completion in 1983. In this report we will describe the plan we had conceived to administer the grant, what we learned through administering the grant for four years, and the impact the program has had on our institution's commitment to excellence in teaching. Our intention is to describe what worked well in the hope that some of our experiences can be applied to faculty development programs on other campuses.

The Institutional Ethos

Indiana University is the eighth largest institution of higher education in the United States. The oldest and largest of the campuses,

P. A. Lacey (Ed.). *Revitalizing Teaching Through Faculty Development.* New Directions for Teaching and Learning, no. 15. San Francisco: Jossey-Bass, September 1983.

Bloomington, enrolls over 30,000 students in a full spectrum of under-graduate, graduate, and professional programs. The campus charac-terizes itself and is nationally regarded as a research institution. Its fac-ulty are recipients of an array of prestigious honors and awards in research, and the university actively supports several resource agencies for scholars, including the Office of Research and Graduate Develop-ment and the campus-wide Institute for Advanced Study.

Although the university places a strong emphasis on research, there is also a quiet affirmation of teaching at Indiana. The importance of teaching has always been reflected in the tacit norms, formal poli-cies, and specific programs that support and recognize good teaching. A number of university administrators won teaching awards before their appointments to administrative posts, so there was reason to expect support for programs that stress the importance of good teach-ing. Indeed, the university's proposal for a postdoctoral teaching fel-lows program originated with the desire of the dean of faculties and the vice president to promote good teaching. Shortly after the chief executive officer of the Bloomington campus, the associate dean of faculties, and representatives of the Lilly Endowment met early in 1979, the dean developed a draft of a proposal and asked our office, the Division of Development and Special Projects of the Audio-Visual Center (DDSP), to assist with the proposal and manage the grant if it were awarded. The progression of interest in the fellowship program is important because it shows where support, a fundamental issue in the development of such innovations, came from within the university administration.

A History of Support for Teaching

The administration's expressed interest in good teaching can also be seen in formal university politics. It was and still is university policy that, in order to attain tenure, each faculty member must dem-onstrate adequacy in teaching, research, and service and be clearly outstanding in one of these areas. The norms of the institution are such that the safest route to tenure has been to demonstrate excellence in research. This has led to some faculty cynicism about the possibility for advancement through excellence in teaching. The administration's response to this cynicism has been the consistent and even application of university policy, but two important variables have created the cur-rent state of affairs: Each department may weigh the criteria in accor-dance with its own goals, and documentation in the area of teaching has been uneven and often inadequate. Therefore, decision making has been heavily influenced by the area that can be most precisely measured — productivity in research and publications. The administration hoped that the teaching fellows program, by focusing on the problems of assessing good teaching, would provide the means to help individuals improve their own teaching and departments document excellence in teaching when faculty members face review for tenure.

Another indication of the university's concern for excellence in teaching has always been found in the many special programs offered to faculty in this area. The agencies designed to assist instructors in improving their teaching include the Audio-Visual Center, Radio-Television Services, Bloomington Academic Computing Service, Bureau of Testing and Evaluative Studies, the Office of Learning Resources, and the Teaching Resources Center in the College of Arts and Sciences. In addition, faculty could consult with staff at the Learning Skills Center and University Division, which are both designed to meet the academic needs of undergraduate students. These many teaching agencies were neither coordinated by a single administration before the teaching fellows' grant was awarded nor had they ever had occasion to sit down in the same room and plot common strategies. There simply was no history of collective action.

The introduction of the teaching fellows program, then, could not have been better timed. The raw materials, and the inclination to put them at the disposal of those who wished to improve their teaching, were at hand. The program provided the catalyst for institutional renewal and made it clear that teaching norms, policies, and programs needed to be better articulated and coordinated.

Goals of the Program

The goals of the program were threefold: They addressed the needs of the individual, the department, and the institution. The following are some excerpts from the original proposal.

Goals for Individual Awardee

We believe that the route to excellent teaching is a highly individualized matter; thus our program emphasizes individualized approaches to improved teaching effectiveness. *The program should enable each fellow to develop proficiency in a number of important aspects of teaching in a pattern suited to the faculty member's discipline and departmental needs as well as the individual's own values of teaching and learning.*

Departmental Goals

The... program is planned so as to influence the fellow's departmental context as well as the fellow's own ideas, motivations, and competence. *We are convinced that without a supportive climate within the department it is difficult for the faculty member to sustain newly learned views and skills in teaching.*

A supportive departmental context probably consists of several elements — visible, coherent policies on teaching that are articulated by both the chairperson and the senior leadership of the department; systematic efforts to appraise the quality of teaching in the department; the allocation of resources to support good teaching; and frequent opportunities for collegial dialogue concerning teaching. By enlisting the support of each fellow's chairperson, by involving a senior colleague or mentor in the program, and in some cases requesting departmental funds, we emphasized the idea that in effective teaching the processes of teaching must be shaped by the academic context and its significance for the student.

Institutional Goals

The... program will have a significant impact on the Bloomington campus in terms of clarifying and strengthening institutional support for faculty development efforts. The... program will be planned and publicized so as to increase campus-wide interest in teaching and demonstrate in one more way that efforts toward good teaching are rewarded.

In retrospect, we believe the decision to divide the program goals into three separate areas was a sound one. Our program emphasized individual development and support and excluded many group activities. This focus differed from that of other postdoctoral teaching fellows programs. Our previous experience had shown that faculty often show little tolerance for groups that foster unstructured discussion of pedagogical principles or for programs that feature group projects, designated readings, or weekly seminars on subjects chosen by the directors. Therefore, we sacrificed group activities for individual flexibility. Although we stressed individual projects, we did meet monthly as a group, and those meetings gave fellows the chance to exchange information informally and linked them to established teaching networks.

We saw the development of links between our office and academic departments as crucial to the program's success. We discovered that the young faculty members often were unable to make full use of their fellowship support: In some cases, departments assigned them to extra service on departmental committees because they had less than a full teaching load. But, for the program to work, the fellows must have actual released time that the department cannot, in effect, take back by increasing the faculty members' service load. In order to free faculty members from some of these imposed encumbrances, we found that we had to visit a number of department chairs to discuss what the program was doing for the fellows' professional growth; we had to show the chairs how the models that we were developing for documenting the participating faculty members' teaching would help the department make a good case at the tenure review for retaining faculty members on the basis of excellence in teaching.

We believed that increasing campus awareness of the teaching fellows program and heightening interest in improving teaching might be the first steps toward institutional change. We hoped that the program would provide the impetus to coordinate the offices of teaching resources and to make these agencies more visible. By mustering these resources, we wanted to make clear that teaching and research are missions of equal value at the university. We hoped to involve the campus administration and faculty in the general teaching activities (conferences and lectures) planned for the fellows. Finally, we encouraged the fellows to exercise leadership in departmental and campus affairs as spokespersons for good teaching.

Structure of the Program

We have emphasized some differences between our goals and those of other Lilly-funded programs, but all such programs share certain structural elements. Each has funded eight to fifteen fellows a year. Each has had an identifiable director. Fellows received released time from their academic duties, usually 50 percent of their total teaching commitment for an academic year. Most programs sponsored fellows in work on individual projects, and they were expected to attend two national conferences administered by the Lilly Endowment each year. Fellows were expected to meet regularly as a group, and to write a letter about their experiences to the Lilly Endowment at about the midpoint in each academic year. While our program shared all these usual and fundamental elements, our goals—support and flexibility for individuals interested in improving their teaching styles, help for the department seeking to document good teaching, and impetus for the renewal of the university's commitment to good teaching — were intended to reflect the particular milieu at Indiana University.

Moves to Ensure Success

A number of public and semi-public actions were initiated by the first notice of the award and, to a degree, repeated each year the award was continued. These were carefully orchestrated to emphasize all three goal levels for the program: individual, departmental, and institutional. Every possible candidate was contacted. We created opportunities for each of the service agencies to make meaningful contributions to the program planning activities and used our network of significant campus leaders to act as advocates for the program. Each prospective candidate received a personal letter from the Dean of Faculties, which proved to be an effective tool for recruiting many of the fellows. We also used all forms of public media to publicize the grant. Public meetings were held that were reasonably successful. The local news media were quite cooperative, although it was difficult to sell the newsworthiness of teaching awards. Eventually, we were able to develop a large number of feature articles about the accomplishments of the fellows.

The support of former fellows was most important in successful recruitment. In fact, we found that former fellows were the severest judges of new talent. They appeared to value the process so much that they were not about to reward or encourage individuals who could not meet the same high standards they had set for themselves. However, if we had it to do again, we would invest more of our energies into personal discussions with a wide range of campus leaders besides former program participants. Two or three campus leaders were responsible for recruiting at least twelve of our fellows.

Criteria of Selection

Each year we revised our criteria of selection and developed hypotheses about which departments or school environments would contribute to successful teaching development. Some departments placed a very high premium on research. For example, we had a limited number of applicants from hard sciences or mathematics, in which younger faculty members often need postdoctoral fellowships to support their research. Through discussion with faculty, we discovered that nearly all faculty who progress through the ranks in the hard sciences receive postdoctoral fellowships of some sort to support research. In addition, young faculty in these departments spend the first two or three years establishing a laboratory. Therefore, most of them were unwilling to give time to a teaching improvement program at the expense of the research programs that are necessary for faculty survival in the hard sciences. Likewise, we were unwilling to intrude because the costs for these junior faculty might be too high.

However, we found one department that stood out as an exception to the above pattern. Over the four years, a disproportionate number of psychology faculty participated in the fellowship program. Young faculty members in psychology also depend on postdoctoral support to complete the laboratory research that is important in their discipline. But the first teaching fellows from the Psychology Department found that they were able to make genuine progress in the development of their teaching careers without taking away time from their research activities. Most fellows thought the key to the program's success was in the large blocks of uninterrupted time they had to reflect on both areas. These fellows were also successful in receiving early promotions. What had been perceived as a liability in the other sciences — that is, less time for research — became an asset in psychology.

In the humanities, where the standards are certainly as rigorous and expectations for performance equally as high as in the sciences, we found that the tradition of scholarship, research, and writing already provided a better fit with the goals of the teaching fellows program. Young humanists found it quite normal and natural to propose an individual project and seek consultation when necessary.

A General Profile of the Teaching Fellows

The individual project goals and styles of teaching and learning have varied so much among the teaching fellows that it is difficult to speak about them collectively. There have been forty-four fellows — eight senior faculty funded by the institution and thirty-six junior faculty funded by the Lilly Endowment. Their departmental affiliations cover every major unit within the university. There have been fellows from the arts, humanities, and social sciences, a few senior faculty in hard sciences, and several from the professional schools.

The initial focus was on nontenured, junior faculty in their first years as college teachers. After the second year of the program, we were delighted to find senior faculty members expressing a desire to improve their teaching and during the final two years of the program the university provided additional money to support several senior faculty fellows. The recruitment of senior faculty indicated an institutional recognition of the fact that good teaching is a continuing achievement and requires sustained effort. Their participation also helped validate concern for teaching among junior faculty.

Elements of the Program

Throughout the four years of the teaching fellows program, we have developed and refined several elements that we feel make our program uniquely suited to our university's particular needs. They include establishing a relationship between the individual fellow and a consultant which we call the "contracting process," extended luncheon meetings, and teaching conferences that bring together faculty from all disciplines and every regional campus.

Individual Support. The exchange between a fellow and a consultant in DDSP has provided the basis for the support our program gives each participant. The consultant first helps the fellow define and refine goals for the fellowship year. This relationship between a fellow and the consultant (who may be a staff member or an advanced graduate student) challenges the fellow to examine and articulate his or her goals in particular courses. As a result, the fellow often begins to look more closely at his or her ideas about teaching and learning. With these concerns before them, the consultant and the fellow draw up a contract that lays out the steps by which the fellow will try to accomplish a goal. This goal may be as broad as working to build a course and a teaching style around certain ideas about teaching and learning, or as specific as designing a computer-based instructional program. As part of this plan, fellows are encouraged to examine their professional goals and to plan the desired direction of their careers. The substance of the plan or contract focuses on teaching development, but the contract also touches on their future plans; thus, the resource personnel can better understand the fellows' professional goals in their entirety.

A typical contract outlines the goals of the project, describes specific activities that the fellow will undertake to reach those goals, lists university resources needed to complete the project, projects the tangible results of the project, and often lays out a timetable for the progress of the work. However, the contract is only part of the fellow's continuing discussion with his or her consultant. The consultants can put resources that a project requires at the fellow's disposal. Consultants for some projects have coordinated the fellow's contracts with as many as fifty staff members from various resource agencies.

Fellows credit the continuing relationship with the consultant —

which by no means ends when the contract is drawn up—with helping them to clarify goals, plan their time, and bring the projects to fruition. The fellows have developed and redesigned courses, produced computer-based instructional programs, and prepared a number of audiovisual aids for teaching, as well as carrying away with them a new command of the wide range of teaching resources. Almost all junior faculty have also developed a means of assessing and documenting the effectiveness of their own teaching. The procedures for collecting this data include interviews with the fellows and their students, videotaping, evaluation by peers, ratings by students, observation in the classroom, and self-assessment. The models our office and the fellows have created can help all faculty to examine their teaching as part of their professional development. And with more and better documentation, it is possible for review committees to take effective teaching more seriously as a criterion for promotion and tenure.

Group Activities. The projects undertaken by the teaching fellows in our program make it different from other programs that include many more group seminars and arranged presentations that revolve around participants' individual work. When the fellows did meet as a group, they worked together to sharpen their effectiveness in tackling institutional problems. Luncheon meetings provided an ideal place and time for fellows to meet and discuss solutions to general problems, such as institutional and departmental policies and attitudes toward the importance of teaching.

The first year's fellows developed a cohesiveness and a sense of identity as "Lilly Fellows" that made them increasingly influential during the year in working with departments and with the administration. Over the four years, the fellowship groups extended luncheon invitations to a number of influential campus administrators, senior faculty, mentors, and past fellows. They invited a panel of department chairpersons to discuss the need for increased support of interdisciplinary teaching. They asked the Dean and Associate Dean of Faculties to discuss why most of the fellows' young colleagues did not believe teaching was rewarded. They assembled prestigious senior faculty who had served on promotion and tenure committees to offer suggestions for developing the teaching dossier, and invited mentors and past fellows to compare strategies for influencing departmental policies toward teaching. Through these discussions with campus leaders, fellows gained an understanding of how university decisions and policies related to teaching were formulated. As a direct result, one fellow was appointed to the College Curriculum Committee and several others to departmental and campus teaching committees. At the same time, university administrators and senior faculty usually left with a better sense of the concerns of junior, nontenured faculty. The lasting effect of all these discussions was an active support system that coalesced around the central theme of teaching.

Conferences. Institutional interest and support for good teaching was increased through yearly, system-wide conferences. At the start of the second fellowship year, the fellows decided to invite William G. Perry from Harvard University to talk about "Intellectual and Ethical Development in the College Years." They extended invitations to all Bloomington campus faculty, and the response was so positive that they decided to invite faculty throughout the entire Indiana University system. The number of conference registrants from the whole University system increased even more in 1982 for a program on "The Improvement and Evaluation of Teaching," featuring John Centra, a senior researcher from the Educational Testing Service, and Kenneth Eble, a professor of English from the University of Utah. During the most recent conference on "Teaching and Computers," which featured Richard Van Horn, provost at Carnegie-Mellon University, and John McCredie, president of EDUCOM, administrators from the offices of the dean of faculties, vice president, and president assumed leadership roles. Faculty involvement in the conferences has been significant, with past and present fellows serving on the planning committees and presenting workshops. But, more importantly, administrative support for the program and effective teaching in general has become more visible with each conference.

Faculty Views of the Program

After the first year of the Indiana program we began to explore ways in which the faculty perceived their fellowship experiences and found that there seemed to be five elements that contributed to participants' satisfaction. First, the released time was absolutely crucial to the success of the program. We have noted that, in various ways, Indiana University is a research institution; in that context, the internal and external rewards for progress in teaching development have to exceed the costs. The large blocks of uninterrupted time, which the program made available to fellows, was a sufficient enticement for most of those who first considered applying for the award, and after the first year it became an attractive benefit for new fellows. In many cases, both the teaching and research activities of young fellows flourished during the fellowship year. As one fellow reported:

The primary benefit of the fellowship to me can be summarized in two words — free time. Freedom from the intense competition between laboratory commitments on one hand and lecture time on the other has given me an opportunity to see new connections between various issues and findings in my particular research area and the more general concepts I attempt to communicate in the classroom. In short, this sabbatical-like period has given me time to freshen my perspective on both teaching and research and to recognize heretofore untapped and unappreciated relationships between them.

A second element that gave fellows satisfaction in the program was the consultation process. At the start of each year, many of the fellows viewed the consultants as curious appendages to the fellowship process — as polite and amiable people who could be safely ignored if they became burdensome. It therefore became extremely important to demonstrate our skill as consultants in the first weeks of the fellowship year. The following comment illustrates how the relationship between consultants and fellows developed over time.

> At first I thought, how can someone who doesn't know a thing about law help me, but it's turned out that she is able to draw comparisons between various legal doctrines that I hadn't really seen. She's also acted sort of like a genie in a bottle. I'd ask her to find what films had been done on legal topics and she'd come back in a week with catalogues and useful suggestions on how to integrate media in the course.

The consultant had to be assertive at critical junctures throughout the year in order to keep up the momentum, to challenge assumptions, and help the fellow think through particularly knotty problems. In most cases, the relationship between the program participants and the consultant became a central part of the fellowship year. Fellows felt that an important collaborative arrangement had been developed that contributed to their personal growth.

A third element that contributed to faculty satisfaction was the sense that they had become a part of a network of successful teachers. We underestimated the positive effects of this aspect of the program. When we first put the young fellows in contact with campus leaders — when they began to interact across disciplines and professional orientations and used the networks of their mentors to share teaching information — it was as if they had developed an entirely new concept of teaching. As one fellow noted, "It was as if I had entered into a secret or at least a transparent society that had been quietly operating for years and had suddenly opened to me through the vehicle of the Fellowship." After the first year or two, the achievements of the early fellows attracted and encouraged those fellows supported in subsequent years. Some of them achieved early promotion and others received awards for being outstanding teachers. In one case, a fellow was promoted on the basis of excellence in teaching, the first case in the history of that department.

Fourth, the fellows were also pleased to find that they were part of a national movement of faculty who were concerned about teaching. Many of the faculty approached the required national conference reluctantly, full of suspicions that they would be harangued by educators throughout a weekend of tedious lectures. Fortunately, the Lilly Endowment's long experience with conferences enabled them to bring in leaders who were stimulating speakers and provoked substantial intellectual exchange. Most of the fellows found they were quietly caught up in the atmosphere of the weekend and their suspicions were dispelled. Many lasting relationships developed across programs. Guarded expectations were replaced by the sense that teaching was a vital, even revolutionary, force in the threatening and resource-poor decade of the 1980s. As one fellow reported, "The conferences were instructive for me; they afforded an opportunity to learn about other colleagues' fields and special interests, to discuss with these colleagues problems of mutual concern, and to hear fresh perspectives on teaching and learning."

Finally, many fellows found that their self-concepts as teaching scholars underwent a transformation. They initially had a sense that the institution insulated them in a cocoon where, through extraordinary effort and perhaps a little bit of luck, a metamorphosis would take place and a few would be allowed to emerge into a new life of intellectual freedom and productivity. The following comment illustrates the changes in one fellow's perception of himself as a teacher.

> When I finished graduate school I was already a competent researcher. However, I was prepared to be little more than a miserable teacher. After two years in the classroom I have, at the very least, developed some appreciation for the characteristics of a good teacher, although I have not always succeeded in putting this knowledge to good use. The. . . fellowship has allowed me to cognitively collate these two years' worth of experiences in

preparation for returning to the classroom with increased self-confidence, renewed vigor, a rediscovered enthusiasm for teaching, and a new corpus of knowledge.

Ironically enough, the unusual level of sincere interest in the junior professors involved, the easy access to all of the resources needed to complete projects, and the myriad of alternatives that consultants presented seemed to overwhelm the fellows in the first months of the program. One of the most intriguing signs of this was that many found it difficult to spend the two-hundred-dollar stipend that was set aside for personal support—for books, teaching, materials, computer programming, and so on. In addition, many of the fellows expressed concern about "life after Lilly." Recently, one young faculty member told us, "I know that you told me that the support would be there after the fellowship year. I just want you to know that it was and that I am surprised. I really feel that I've accomplished something." We are still not certain whether this comment says more about the stress of being a nontenured faculty member or if our program was particularly effective in providing opportunities for professional development.

Conclusion: Other Successful Developments

In addition to the favorable responses to the program from sponsored faculty members, we can identify other developments over the four-year term of the grant that reflected or contributed to the growing success of the program. First of all, the fellows became significant advocates for teaching. Almost immediately, some program participants became leaders in their departments or school teaching committees, by either election or appointment. Perhaps this phenomenon speaks most to the quality of junior faculty in our institution and their ability to lead. In retrospect we are certainly well pleased with our selection processes. Another sign of the growing success of the program was the extensive sharing of teaching information among fellows and their colleagues. Within a year, many of the fellows were giving public presentations on teaching issues, sharing the processes of career planning developed for the grant, and disseminating information about teaching agencies. In most cases we felt these informal activities, although less visible, were far more important than their formal advocacy on committees. Fellows became day-to-day spokespersons for good teaching.

Yet another reflection of the growing influence of this communication network can be seen in the interest faculty have shown in our teaching conferences. The first year we had visible support from the dean of faculties and dean of learning resources and 200 faculty attended. In the second year the chief executive officers of the Bloomington campus gave a keynote address on dossier development and 300 faculty were present. In the third year, the president of the university was a participant in the planning and presentation of the program. For this most recent conference we had nearly 500 faculty registrants, and we were forced to turn away more than 150 others.

The campus perception of the teaching fellows also contributed to the growing success of the program. Some of the fellows were promoted early, and in many cases demonstrated excellence in research as well as in teaching. Tangible signs of personal rewards, as well as support by university administrators and others, seemed to enhance the image of teaching fellows as successful teachers and scholars. But the final, and perhaps most significant, development over the four-year term of the grant award, has been an institutional commitment to future faculty development programs. Efforts to reorganize and coordinate the teaching resource agencies seem to have provided the initial impetus for change. The Lilly grant brought together the directors of these teaching agencies for the first time, with the expressed purpose of coordinating resources for the fellows. Before long, the directors and the dean of faculties began to meet periodically, not only to discuss teaching fellows' projects but also to share resources and staff for other teaching programs. Both individual and collaborative projects have been highly successful because of this new-found ability to integrate resources for the improvement of teaching.

Thomas M. Schwen is director of both the Audio-Visual Center and the Lilly postdoctoral teaching awards program at Indiana University, Bloomington.

Mary Deane Sorcinelli is associate director of the Lilly postdoctoral teaching awards program at Indiana University, Bloomington.

An effective faculty development program must be politically astute. It must recognize the faculty member's commitments to an academic discipline and to research, as well as to effective teaching and seek to support activities that enhance these commitments.

The Politics of Vitalizing Teaching

Paul A. Lacey

Erik Erikson says humans are the teaching species. It is fundamental to our nature that we live among overlapping generations of people who must teach one another. We are also the learning species. We are taught to drink from a cup and eat from a spoon, to be toilet-trained, to speak and later perhaps to write, to cross streets, to say please, and perhaps even ride a bike or later drive a car. Some things we have natural aptitudes for, like standing up and walking. If walking had to be taught, more than one teacher has said, millions of human beings would never learn how.

Interwoven with all the informal teaching and learning that goes on throughout our lives is the formal schooling process that takes us from basic skills and a wide range of subjects to higher levels of study and fewer subjects. College teachers, who are what they are in large part because they always did well in formal learning, have gone through all the stages of formal schooling. The person who starts teaching in a college, Ph.D. or ABD, in addition to all of those other teaching and learning experiences, has been taught a discipline that involves a large content and a language for talking about the discipline—for distinguishing it from or establishing its links with other areas of study. It also

P. A. Lacey (Ed.). *Revitalizing Teaching Through Faculty Development.* New Directions for Teaching and Learning, no. 15. San Francisco: Jossey-Bass, September 1983.

includes methods for making the discipline yield up its significance and ways of knowing what constitutes valid research. The college teacher potentially has an extraordinarily complex, rich composite picture of what a teacher looks like and does, or at least should look like and do.

The teaching-learning process is like the elephant in the Indian fable, and we who are teachers and learners are like the blind men — each knowing something about the subject, but no one knowing enough by himself; all of us have to make the fullest possible sense of the process by sharing our limited information.

How We Get Started

As a college sophomore I took a course in mathematical logic that was a liberating experience for me. For the first time since eighth grade I had a fresh start at mathematics, and I found I could understand and do the work satisfactorily. Years later I told my instructor, who was a graduate student in philosophy when he taught the class, how much I had benefited from the course. He told me that what he particularly remembered about the course was that he was assigned to teach it with just a day's notice. His specialty was not logic, and he recalled ending virtually every class with the words, "I don't know, but I'll find out and tell you tomorrow." My instructor did not think highly of his teaching or of the assigned text — and I was a math moron — yet from that unlikely mixture some fine teaching-learning occurred. But what could my instructor or I, even then destined to become a teacher, have learned about teaching from that course?

When we newly-appointed teaching fellows met to talk about our duties, we received some advice from a kindly, urbane graduate dean that he had received from his mentor at the start of his own teaching career: Always look over your notes before going into class and avoid sarcasm with students. That was all the dean believed he could offer us, but it was excellent advice as far as it went. One of the finest teachers I know — his students say so and I have watched him in class — said his best advice came from his mother, who had received it from her teacher in normal school: You have not said anything until you have said it three times and, once again, there is no place for sarcasm in the classroom. Of course, we know that other mentors give different kinds of advice about teaching: Never let them call you by your first name; hold strictly to your office hours; never ask if there are any questions; do not let teaching take time away from your own work; change your pace every twenty minutes; write your key points on the blackboard. Some of that advice is deeply humane, but some is deeply cynical.

Some of it has a nuts-and-bolts pragmatism about it, or emphasizes doing justice to the discipline or doing justice primarily to the students or oneself. Clearly, not all of the suggestions have equal value.

The Politics of Teaching

To speak of the politics of vitalizing teaching is to acknowledge the complexity of things represented by all that advice. According to Aristotle, we express our gregarious nature through *politics*. It is how we adjudicate among and reconcile the conflicting claims of justice — in this case, justice to ourselves, to our students, to our colleagues, and to our discipline. We must begin, then, by taking seriously both the conventional and the unconventional wisdom about teaching. Some basic — and ingrown — attitudes about teaching that need to be addressed appear below.

- Teaching is an innate talent, not something to be learned. It is more like walking, which just comes to us, than it is like reading and writing, which we learn by drill and practice.
- Teaching is content-less, so what is taught about teaching is not true subject matter. At worse, it is a lot of gimmicks obscured by pretentious jargon.
- Teaching is simply a matter of knowing a field of study well. The more you know about the subject, the better you will teach. Teaching cannot be separated from scholarship because, in essence, it is only your knowledge of an area conveyed to apprentices in the field instead of your peers. (No discussion about good teaching can occur in our profession without tribute being paid to some crusty, harsh, old curmudgeon who hated his students, or someone else who could never be heard even in the front row. "In conventional terms he was a terrible teacher, but he was a great scholar who taught me more than anyone else I had.")
- Teaching is personal brilliance, usually in the form of brilliant monologue. (Mark Harris' novel *Wake Up, Stupid!* [1959] includes a vivid example of this. The protagonist is hiring a new instructor who must begin by teaching three courses in freshman English. "Teachers who are dullards will find such courses dull," he says, "but you, I suspect, will transform them into surveys of W. Wycherly Wood, I, W. Wycherly Wood, II, and W. Wycherly Wood, III... for freshmen, a gentleman as quick as you ought to be able to cook up an hour's bright conversation from what the man

before you left on the blackboard" [pp. 178–179].) Besides, students would not know good teaching if they saw it. They do not have the expertise to judge a teacher's competence in the discipline, so they only really judge qualities of personality. "Good teaching" thus means being popular with students, entertaining, light-weight, and an easy grader.

- Bad teaching cannot hurt good students. (Jeremy Bernstein reports in *The American Scholar* (1982–83), "I. I. Rabi once remarked to me that nascent physicists seem able to survive any amount of bad teaching. Rabi hever had, at least until he received his Ph.D., anyone he can recall who was a good teacher.") We who are in the profession may have been dazzled by the brilliant lecturer, captivated by the scholarly devotion of the curmudgeon, or simply uninjured by the dreadful teachers. Somehow we were taught and learned. We fell in love with a subject, with a way of life and thought, and we pursued it, regardless of the quality of teaching we received.
- Teaching is the price we pay for doing our own work — research. Research is where the deepest stimulation and greatest academic rewards are. We should pay the costs with genuine coin, but, as with taxes, we are not obliged to pay more than the minimum that we owe.

However, beyond all this disagreement — and prejudice, defensiveness, and shrewd observation of reality about what teaching is — there are some practical conditions with which anyone must work who wishes to create a positive "political" climate for focusing attention on teaching, identifying what makes teaching effective, and supporting people who want to improve their own teaching. According to the Ladd-Lipset survey (1978), most university and college professors think of themselves as teachers more than as researchers. According to a University of Michigan study of twenty-four institutions of higher education (Blackburn and others, 1980), an overwhelming majority of faculty say that they value teaching very highly. They also believe they teach well, but that their colleagues may not value teaching as highly or do it as well. About 90 percent of the faculty members surveyed judged themselves to be above average or superior as teachers; when students are asked to judge faculty as teachers, they place about 90 percent of the faculty they come in contact with in the same way. So, in general, neither faculty nor students believe there are serious problems with the quality of college teaching.

Furthermore, college teachers surveyed overwhelmingly identify knowing the discipline as the most important aspect of teaching.

They view teaching as primarily transmission of knowledge and infor-mation — "What emerges, then, is a picture of the academic as expert" (Blackburn and others, 1980, p. 40). They value the qualities that go into making good lectures: control of material, precision in handling data, coherence of argument and presentation, and stimulation of fur-ther thought in the hearers. The well-crafted lecture is an act of homage to all that constitutes a discipline: content, method, standards of judg-ment, rules of evidence, and the best scholarly models. Anything that seems to separate the intellectual enterprise of the discipline from the process of teaching and learning will therefore be regarded by many faculty with deep suspicion — and seen as trivial, subversive, or intellec-tually dishonest.

University and college faculty correctly perceive that their insti-tutions reward research and publication more than they do classroom performance. They also believe that their own intellectual development is best furthered by the intense, focused, high order of scholarly activi-ties that are usually identified with research. But it matters to faculty how their students perform. Student ratings mean less to them than informal feedback from respected students and how students do on papers and examinations. Faculty determine how good their teaching is largely by self-assessment and student performance and much less by how their colleagues or administrators view their teaching (Blackburn and others, 1980).

The Politics of Institutional Support for Teaching

A successful faculty development program to support teaching will not get far by looking for opponents to vanquish. Instead, it should focus on what is called, in politics, *coalition building* — identifying impor-tant common interests that can best be met by working with others on the broadest levels. Another common word for this activity is *networking*. A politically astute program acknowledges, respects, and plays to fac-ulty strengths and should not be perceived as looking for weaknesses to overcome or errors to rid itself of. It assumes that faculty see them-selves as concerned, effective teachers and seeks to build support groups based on that foundation.

Since most faculty already feel strong tensions between the claims of research and the claims of teaching in their careers, an astutely designed program should not push redressing the balance in teaching's favor as part of its agenda. Instead, it encourages faculty to find ways to make research and teaching mutually supportive, since, in most direct competitions between the two, teaching will lose. And a successful program should be pragmatic rather than ideological in emphasis. It is not a repository for right answers about effective teaching but a place to explore a faculty member's individual questions. For example, it should not deprecate lecturing as a bad teaching method or disparage disciplinary commitments in favor of multidisciplinary teaching. Instead, it will address the needs that teachers themselves bring forward.

An astutely designed program takes faculty members' deepest intellectual commitments seriously. In practice, that means granting the discipline paramount importance and inviting the teacher to describe his or her goals in terms of content and method that are presented to and mastered by students. Over time, a faculty member engaged in consultation about teaching may want to address other kinds of questions — including the developmental needs of students or the intellectual stimulation of multidisciplinary study — but the agenda should originate with the faculty member, not the consultant. A teacher's continued or renewed excitement about his or her discipline should be taken as a positive indicator of vital teaching.

It is fortunate that most faculty members see student performance as a measure of their own teaching effectiveness. (Apparently even the most resolute monologist likes some evidence that the audience valued the performance.) Faculty should be encouraged to take student ratings seriously as a source of information about improving student as well as teacher performance. This might lead to devising new evaluation instruments, adding questions to a standard instrument, interviewing students about what they have learned, consulting with a trusted colleague about what the ratings mean, or any combination of these actions. A program that offers these services, at the request of a faculty member, with the explicit purpose of getting better performance out of the students, has begun on solid ground.

Helping junior faculty find their place in the profession should be a major focus for any faculty development program. This entails encouraging the junior person to make connections with the appropriate senior colleagues, role models, and mentors. It means helping the junior person to understand the broadest possible conceptions of professionalism that are consonant with his or her own personality and the constraints of the institution. Any particular faculty development program has to be concerned with supporting and keeping the right people for its own institution, but something is also owed to the whole educational community. A good faculty development program must also serve the person who belongs in teaching but will not gain tenure in a particular department of a particular university.

Elements of a Program

Most suggestions for creating a faculty development program begin, "First, get a grant"—good but not necessarily the most practical of advice. Outside funding support for faculty development activities has diminished over the years, as has discretionary money from within university budgets. Any college or university now trying to support effective teaching is more likely to be faced with the problem of putting something coherent together out of bits and pieces of programs spread throughout the institution. The political considerations of such a plan can only be acknowledged here, not addressed with any concrete practical advice. What can be addressed is the range of practical activities that motivate the development of faculty programs to support teaching. Comprehensive programs typically offer the following kinds of activities, orchestrated in various arrangements: workshops, conferences, and seminars that are on or off campus; classroom visitation; videotaping of classes; collecting of student evaluation data through questionnaires and interviews; individual consultations with experts on various aspects of teaching and learning; support for course design projects or new teaching methods; and grants for leaves or released time to work on teaching projects.

Some of these activities are relatively low-cost. On-campus workshops, conferences, and seminars organized around a topic of local interest can draw on resident experts for demonstrations and presentations and give participants opportunities to establish valuable connections with like-minded colleagues. What distinguishes a workshop from a conference or seminar is not always clear, but planners of a group activity ought to consider both what they hope to accomplish and what expectations are raised by describing an event in each way. Workshops frequently stress hands-on experience with such things as new teaching or research methods and devices: for example, Computer-Assisted Instruction, designing and using audiovisual materials, or introducing Programmed Self-Instruction in a classroom. In such workshops, after a relatively brief time, the participants get an introduction to a new teaching aid, practice it enough to have some confidence about going on with it, and can develop the beginnings of associations with colleagues and experts who might help encourage further experimentation. The practicality of such workshops is perhaps their greatest comfort to the novice. They are utilitarian and therefore essentially non-intellectual, so they pose no threat to a participant's basic intellectual or disciplinary commitments. Consequently, one can participate in them at low risk.

Another kind of workshop is more inspirational than practical. They may include "hands-on" self-reflective, role-playing, and simulation activities, or the emphasis may be on presentations from master teachers about their own solutions to teaching-learning problems and discussions about why people went into the profession. The practical suggestions that come out of this kind of workshop usually have more to do with finding integrity in one's professional and personal life than with choosing the best software for a course module. Therefore, this kind of workshop can seem more directly focused on a teacher's emotional commitments to and feelings about the profession and consequently is of higher risk to many faculty. Purely motivational or inspirational workshops are often dismissed as "touchy-feely" by large numbers of teachers, and both organizers and participants are often viewed with suspicion as anti-intellectuals.

Conferences and seminars can be organized in ways that are familiar and therefore of a lower risk to participants; they can be organized around a philosophical or technical problem, a signficant text or set of texts, or a broad intellectual theme. A keynote speaker, other speakers followed by respondents, panels, a closing address, and all of this to be published as a *Proceedings* — the form is so familiar that participants know where they are and can concentrate entirely on the subject matter of the conference or seminar. The faculty member asked to present a paper to her colleagues is taking a controlled risk on relatively familiar ground. What can be done on-campus can also be done, at greater cost, by sending participants off-campus. Here the risks one feels capable of taking may be greater and the associations with colleagues may be just as personally supportive, though of far less political consequence than at one's own university.

Menges (1980) has shown that such workshops and conferences are the most common activity, the least carefully evaluated, and less positively evaluated by faculty than any of the other major kinds of faculty development activities. Nonetheless, there are good reasons to continue using workshops and conferences. They can be both low-cost and low-risk. They offer people a first chance to announce that they are interested in teaching and learning issues or a specific device or method. They bring people together in new configurations, out of which support groups, associations with colleagues, and networks of experts can emerge. They affirm the professional gifts of resident experts. They reinforce commitment to important professional activities and allow for participants to broaden their own understanding of significant activities. And they give junior faculty experience in planning and organizing professional gatherings and conceiving of ways to frame significant teaching and learning questions.

Another crucial service for a faculty development program to provide is consultation about the meaning of student evalutions. For many faculty, teaching and learning issues become focused when the student evaluations come in. Despite all the assumptions commonly made about them — that they are only perceptions of teaching by uninformed people with a lot of vested interests in easier courses, more generous grading, and so one — faculty know that student evaluations now have an ever-greater influence on renewal, promotion, and tenure decisions. Many faculty also believe that student criticism singles out genuine problems, even if the ways students describe the problems are inaccurate. And some even feel like the student who acknowledges difficulties with analyzing material or writing effectively but does not know how to set about remedying the situation. Therefore, consultation must take on a variety of forms: helping a faculty member interpret patterns of comments or ratings; using the evaluations as a point of entry for discussing course goals and objectives or rethinking the syllabus; arranging for the videotaping of a series of classes for the faculty member to view what occurs in his or her classes; and identifying the teaching strengths perceived by students and the faculty member, and considering ways to enhance those strengths for better teaching and learning. Whereas student evaluations by themselves have relatively little influence on changing a faculty member's behavior, the consultation process can be exceptionally useful in improving an individual's teaching style.

However, such consultation should not ordinarily be prescriptive advice or indoctrination into the consultant's beliefs. It should not even be conventionally supportive or affirming; positive evaluation offered at the wrong time can be damaging, since it puts the consultant in the position of a judge who, pleased this time, could subsequently be displeased. Consultation needs to be confidential and focused primarily on descriptive and analytical tasks. What the faculty member identifies as an issue should be taken as the starting-point for the consultation process. If invited to observe a class, the consultant should ask the instructor to specify anything he wishes to have particularly observed, and the consultant should be rigorous in describing only what she saw and heard. When invited to observe classes, I have found it valuable to attend for two weeks before conversing with the instructor about what I observed. In lecture courses I take notes as though I were a student in the course, bracketing any notes I make about the matters the instructor asked me to observe and report on. In discussion classes I keep notes of what is said, what happened in each fifteen-minute segment of the class, who spoke, and the seating pattern. I give these notes to the instructor so we may discuss, first of all, whether I discerned what the instructor wanted to emphasize. I try to keep all commentary and pre-scriptive judgment out of my notes as much as possible.

A clear description of what one saw in a class can be a powerful aid in helping a faculty member identify what he thinks does and does not work. The conversations that then arise are full of possibilities—but some dangers as well. "What would you do?" is an almost irresistable invitation to unload every bright idea and profound insight into the human condition we have ever had. Of course, there is a place for advice when consulting, but it probably has more effect if it comes late rather than early in the process and if it is couched in *if. . .then* form as much as possible. Sharing what one has seen work in other circum-stances can be helpful, especially if it is offered tentatively, as a bit of experience that might be adapted to a different situation.

Another kind of consultation involves helping faculty think through their resource needs and providing them with information about meeting those needs. Working through a grant proposal, for ex-ample, can be an exceptionally effective way to plan a new course or design a teaching method. Some programs actually administer small grants for course development. More frequently, the faculty develop-ment office helps by keeping track of government, foundation, and uni-versity sources for support; by informing faculty of guidelines and dead-lines; and by putting them in touch with grant development officers and other appropriate university services. Even small amounts of support can provide enormous motivation, as in the case of the teacher in a small college who was bolstered by a five-hundred-dollar grant because it was the first time in twenty years that anyone had bet on his future.

Conclusion

The Lilly postdoctoral teaching fellows program, which sparked all of the chapters in this volume, combined most of the major fea-tures of what a politically astute faculty development program should offer. The two national conferences were a mix of practical and inspira-tional elements; they drew on the expertise of the participants and en-couraged building support systems among participants. They were off-campus and therefore seemed to carry more prestige and less risk. The university programs centered on individual projects, often concerned with course design, for which released or compensated time was pro-vided. In addition, the local groups of fellows met regularly and, in most cases, had mentors or consultants specifically assigned to each of them. Group activities were concerned with common readings, discus-sions, lectures, or demonstrations, and included influential senior colleagues and administrators. Ties among individuals in the programs tended to become strong and long-lasting; fellows reported that though they had no sense of significant collegiality within their own department, they developed friendships with individuals in other departments who shared a commitment to teaching through the fellows program. In addition, consultation and a range of other university services were made available to the fellows. In many cases, the services provided were available to any faculty member, but a teaching program often publicized their availability more widely.

What has been described in this chapter could be facilitated by an outside grant, but many of the fundamental building blocks are already available in most universities. An office that coordinates services and draws people together to explore common interests is a small cost within a university budget but can provide a very great service. More importantly, a politically astute faculty development program is most successful when it takes faculty members' highest aspirations for their professional lives seriously.

References

Bernstein, J. "Science Education for the Nonscientist." *The American Scholar*, Winter 1982–83, 7–12.

Blackburn, R. T., Pellino, G., Boberg, A., and O'Connell, C. "Are Institutional Improvement Programs Off-Target?" In *Improving Teaching and Institutional Quality*. Current Issues in Higher Education, no. 1. Washington, D.C.: American Association of Higher Education, 1980.

Harris, M. *Wake Up, Stupid!* New York: Knopf, 1959.

Ladd, E. C., and Lipset, S. M. *1977 Survey of 4,400 Faculty Members at 161 Colleges and Universities.* Unpublished Survey for *The Chronicle of Higher Education*, 1978.

Menges, R. J. "Teaching Improvement Strategies: How Effective Are They?" In *Improving Education and Institutional Quality.* Current Issues in Higher Education, no. 1. Washington, D.C.: American Association of Higher Education, 1980.

Paul A. Lacey is Bain-Swiggett Professor of English Literature at Earlham College, Richmond, Indiana. He is author of The Inner War: Forms and Themes in Recent American Poetry *(Fortress, 1972). From 1980–83 he was consultant and director for the Lilly Endowment, Inc.'s Postdoctoral Teaching Fellows Program.*

A brief listing of books and articles that may be stimulating to anyone concerned with revitalizing teaching and the larger contexts in which faculty development occurs.

Suggestions for Further Reading

Paul A. Lacey

American Association of Higher Education. *Current Issues in Higher Education.* Nos. 1 and 5. Washington, D.C.: American Association of Higher Education, 1980.

Here are two excellent short collections of presentations from the AAHE annual conference. The first issue includes valuable discussions of measuring the quality of student effort by C. Robert Pace and Alexander W. Astin, respectively. Three other essays of the highest value for faculty development are "Teaching Improvement Strategies: How Effective Are They?" (Robert J. Menges), "Are Instructional Improvement Programs Off-Target?" (Robert T. Blackburn, Glenn Pellino, Alice Boberg, and Colman O'Connell), and "What Are the Obstacles to Improving Quality Teaching?" (Hans O. Maucksch). The fifth issue includes two essays: "Adult Development: A Workable Vision for Higher Education" (Arthur W. Chickering) and "Faculty and Student Development in the 80's: Renewing the Community of Scholars" (L. Lee Knefelkamp).

Astin, A. W. *Four Critical Years: Effects of College on Beliefs, Attitudes, and Knowledge.* San Francisco: Jossey-Bass, 1977.

This study grows from a ten-year survey by the Cooperative Institutional Research Program of the American Council on Education

P. A. Lacey (Ed.). *Revitalizing Teaching Through Faculty Development.* New Directions for Teaching and Learning, no. 15. San Francisco: Jossey-Bass, September 1983.

and University of California at Los Angeles; it uses longitudinal data from over 200,000 students and 300 institutions. Astin discusses student attitudes, self-concepts, aspirations, achievements, and satisfactions with college by contrasting outcomes according to type of institution. Chapters on the permanence of college effects, summary of effects, and implications for policy and practice are especially valuable.

Bergquist, W. H., Gould, R. A., and Greenberg, E. M. *Designing Undergraduate Education.* San Francisco: Jossey-Bass, 1981.

The authors identify six major components of undergraduate programs—time, space, resources, organization, procedures, and outcomes—and divide the book into chapters that address the issues that arise in designing each of those components. The book is full of examples of ways colleges solve the specific problems surrounding each component of undergraduate education. Outcomes—defining intended course and program results—are especially well-addressed.

Bergquist, W., and Phillips, S. R. (Eds.). *A Handbook for Faculty Development,* Vols. 1 and 2. Washington, D.C.: Council of Independent Colleges, 1975, 1977.

Both volumes are filled with ideas, instruments, and plans for faculty development activities. Sample instruments for student evaluations, for life-planning, for course designs, simulations and group activities that focus on teaching and learning issues, personal development, and other facets of faculty development make these volumes among the most practical and stimulating aids in print.

Botkin, J. W., Elmandjra, M., and Malitza, M. *No Limits to Learning: Bridging the Human Gap.* A report to the Club of Rome. New York: Pergamon, 1982.

This is a report to the Club of Rome by scholars from socialist and Third World countries, as well as from the West. It briefly considers some of the global problems facing us—energy, the arms race, and cultural identity—and focuses primarily on the human factors. Can we learn to cope with such problems? Are there ways a whole society can learn to cope with them? The book is especially useful for its discussion of what it calls two main features of innovative learning: anticipatory learning and participatory learning. When one thinks about faculty development and encouragement of effective teaching, it is important to keep in mind the possible connections between effective teaching and learning and coping with global problems. This book and Paulo Freire's *The Pedagogy of the Oppressed* are listed here to provide that larger perspective.

Chickering, A. W., Halliburton, D., Bergquist, W. H., and Lindquist, J.
Developing the College Curriculum: A Handbook for Faculty and Administrators. Washington, D.C.: Council of Independent Colleges, 1977.

The four parts of this book are concerned with curricular rationale, design, practice, and implementation. The authors deal with both theory and practice of curriculum development, the possible innovations, and the research into its effects. The appendices describe specific curricular models, innovative college curricula, and curricula planning tools. This book is especially helpful for programs seeking to address faculty development from an angle other than changing individuals' teaching habits.

Eble, K. E. *The Craft of Teaching: A Guide to Mastering the Professor's Art.* San Francisco: Jossey-Bass, 1976.

There are a few books in which a wise, experienced practitioner of the art of teaching systematically shares the wisdom and experience with the rest of us. Eble's work is one such book. Eble talks about lecturing, leading discussions, assignments, and grading—the nuts and bolts issues of running a course—by constantly referring back and forth from research on teaching to concrete experience. One hears a voice in this book—the witty, musing, reflective voice of a master still intent on improving his own craft.

Ericksen, S. C. *Motivation for Learning: A Guide for the Teacher of the Young Adult.* Ann Arbor: University of Michigan, 1974.

Ericksen, long-time director of the Center for Research on Learning and Teaching at the University of Michigan, brings together research and theoretical findings on such subjects as motivation, learning, social psychology, and personality development to address the practical problems of teaching a course to the young adult. The book has chapters on the student as an individual, defining instructional objectives, attitudes and values of students, and a number of other equally concrete teaching and learning issues.

Freedman, M. (Ed.). *Facilitating Faculty Development.* New Directions for Higher Education, no. 1. San Francisco: Jossey-Bass, 1973.

Freedman gathers eleven essays concerned with faculty development through greater self-awareness and a broader perspective. Essays on the personal histories and professional careers of faculty, on the teacher as artist, and faculty responses to student diversity are to be found here, alongside essays on practical institutional approaches to faculty development. This book comes very early in the history of the faculty development movement of the 1970s, but it is still a goldmine of ideas.

Freire, P. *Pedagogy of the Oppressed.* New York, Seabury, 1970.

This is simply one of the great books about teaching and learning. Freire addresses the problem of how to help the illiterate adult of the Third World overcome the "culture of silence" in which he is submerged. In the process, he offers insights into education as liberation that are applicable at many other levels.

Gullette, M. M. (Ed.). *The Art and Craft of Teaching.* Cambridge, Mass.: Harvard-Danforth Center for Teaching and Learning, 1982.

Nine chapters on some of the most vexing problems of teaching— the first day of class, lecturing, questioning, teaching essay writing, the multifaceted role of the section-leader, the rhythm of the semester, grading, and evaluation. The essays on the rhythm of the semester and the section leader are worth singling out, since the subjects are not often treated in such books, but all the essays are valuable.

Lindquist, J. (Ed.). *Designing Teaching Improvement Programs.* Berkeley, Calif.: Pacific Soundings, 1978.

A sourcebook that is based on pilot projects supported by the W. K. Kellogg Foundation of Battle Creek, Michigan, this book describes what has worked in a number of teaching improvement programs. It addresses practical problems of design, administration, financing and the sustaining of faculty development activities. There are sections specifically addressed to universities, colleges, junior or community colleges, nontraditional and interinstitutional settings.

McKeachie, W. J. *Teaching Tips: A Guidebook for the Beginning College Teacher.* Lexington, Mass.: D.C. Heath, 1969.

What Dr. Spock has been to new parents, McKeachie has been to new college teachers—a practical, down-to-earth guide to the perplexed. Everything is anchored in the most up-to-date research on teaching and learning and directed at the concrete issues of organizing the course. There is even a brief chapter titled, "Getting Students into Seats," which addresses the questions about making a seating plan, taking attendance and dealing with absences. This book claims to be for beginners, but it has something useful to say to anyone concerned with teaching.

Milton, O., and Edgerly, J. W. *The Testing and Grading of Students.* New Rochelle, N.Y.: *Change Magazine,* 1976.

This is one of a series of policy papers published by *Change Magazine* to help faculty become more effective professionals. In its sixty-two pages, this paper examines the fundamental questions of testing, designing tests, grading and interpreting the results of tests, and other forms of evaluation.

Nelsen, W. C., and Siegel, M. E. (Eds.). *Effective Approaches to Faculty Development.* Washington, D.C.: Association of American Colleges, 1980.

A collection of essays by practitioners on professional development, instructional development, curriculum change, organizational development, and consortial approaches to faculty development. There are twenty-three contributors to the collection, representing the widest possible spread of institutions of higher education. There are essays, as well, by faculty participants in faculty development activities. The final section of the book offers assessments of the effectiveness of these programs and future faculty development needs.

Perry, W. G., Jr. *Forms of Intellectual and Ethical Development in the College Years: A Scheme.* New York: Holt, Rinehart and Winston, 1970.

Perry's scheme describes a sequence of "positions" through which college students pass as they go through the college years. The book is based on interviews with college students as they went through their four years of liberal arts education and argues that the forms in which students construe their college experiences characterize the structures that they explicitly or implicitly impute to the world. This is one of the most influential developmental studies of college students in the present literature.

Paul A. Lacey is Bain-Swiggett Professor of English Literature at Earlham College, Richmond, Indiana. He is author of The Inner War: Forms and Themes in Recent American Poetry *(Fortress, 1972). From 1980–83 he was consultant and director for the Lilly Endowment, Inc.'s Postdoctoral Teaching Fellows Program.*

Index